Writing 2

Becoming a Writer

James V. Connell
Mary Enda Costello
Mary Anne Kovacs
Gloria Levine
Joseph Toner

The Center for Learning

Authors

Project director James V. Connell earned his doctorate in curriculum and instruction at Kent State University, Ohio. He is coauthor of five curriculum units in The Center for Learning's language arts series.

Mary Enda Costello, master English teacher and humanities teacher, authored more than a dozen Center for Learning curriculum units. Costello earned her M.A. at the University of Notre Dame, Indiana.

Mary Anne Kovacs, author of many units in The Center for Learning's English and social studies series, earned her M.A. in English from the Bread Loaf School of English, Middlebury College, Vermont. She is an experienced secondary English teacher.

Gloria Levine, who earned her M.A. at the University of California Berkeley, has been a teacher at various levels. Besides writing numerous educational publications, she has served as a Writer's Workshop and Junior Great Books volunteer.

Joseph Toner is an English and social studies teacher with experience at both the elementary and secondary levels. A graduate of Boston College, he received his M.Ed. from Kent State University, Ohio.

The Publishing Team

Rose Schaffer, M.A., President/Chief Executive Officer
Bernadette Vetter, M.A., Vice President
Christine Dresch, M.A., Editor

Cover Design

Susan Chowanetz Thornton, B.S.

List of credits found on Acknowledgments page
beginning on 251.

ISBN-13: 978-1-56077-608-6
ISBN-10: 1-56077-608-0

Contents

Part 6: Persuasion/Argumentation

Part 7: Responding to Literature

Part 8: Across the Curriculum

Part 9: The Student Writer

Introduction

. . . Language is not only a means of communication, it is a primary instrument of thought, a defining feature of culture, and an unmistakable mark of personal identity. Encouraging and enabling students to learn to use language effectively is certainly one of society's most important tasks.

—Professional Summary/Standards
for the English Language Arts, 1996

Writing 2: Becoming a Writer includes forty lessons designed to engage students in the process of writing. As its title suggests, this unit builds on the basic process introduced in *Writing 1* and encourages expanded self-direction. It extends the exposure to diverse composition modes—narration, description, exposition, and persuasion—and addresses the more demanding forms of writing expected in the upper grades, while helping each student develop a personal writing style.

Writing process theory is the foundation for both *Writing 1* and *Writing 2*. The idea that writing is a process—a series of steps, not a simple product—is stressed from beginning to end. According to writing process theory, some or all of the following six steps may be taken (and revisited) in writing any particular piece:

1. Prewriting
   activities geared toward generating topics, ideas, examples, details, and enthusiasm

2. Drafting
   writing an organized first version of a composition with a specific topic, purpose, and audience

3. Conferencing
   oral or written dialogues about the composition (with one or more readers)

4. Revising
   changes and additions to enhance clarity and impact

5. Editing
   correction of errors in grammar, usage, and mechanics

6. Publishing
   composition made available to the intended audience

Throughout the forty lessons in the unit, students are presented with numerous models of good writing, strategies for generating writing topics, suggestions for literary and interdisciplinary connections, and rubrics for guiding and evaluating their writing. They write several essays that visit and revisit the six steps listed above—with revision aided by teacher and peers. Problems in effectiveness of expression are addressed as students work to achieve unity and coherence in their writing—and to find their own voices as writers.

Teacher Notes

How This Unit Is Organized

Writing 2: Becoming a Writer presupposes a basic understanding of the six activities that comprise the writing process. Each of the forty lessons contains a teacher's lesson plan and one or more student handouts. The lessons are grouped into nine parts: Autobiographies; Third-Person Narration; The Problem/Solution Essay; Exposition; Description; Persuasion/Argumentation; Responding to Literature; Across the Curriculum; and The Student Writer.

What Is in Each Lesson

Lessons consist of three parts: Objectives, Notes to the Teacher, and Procedure. The bulleted Objectives should be useful in explaining the purpose of the lesson to students. The Notes to the Teacher section explains the rationale behind the lesson, gives an overview of what teachers and students will be doing, and points out areas that lend themselves to student assessment opportunities. The Notes section also mentions any special materials or preparations that may be needed. The Procedure section suggests specific steps to take in carrying out the lesson (including suggestions for extension and differentiation in a heterogeneous classroom). Sample answers to handout questions are found here.

How to Use This Unit

Each lesson is generally geared for one class period, with a few exceptions. Handouts may be photocopied for distribution to students or made into overhead transparencies for group discussion. The lessons are written so that you may adjust procedures according to specific educational goals, students' needs, and availability of materials and equipment.

Assignments

With any assignment, the emphasis should be on the natural flow of ideas and growth of maturity in writing skills and not on the need the finish an assignment quickly. Homework assignments are included as background or follow-up material. Handouts provide a variety of evaluation tools and activities. In addition, checklists provide guidelines for evaluation of compositions.

Assessment

Teacher evaluation of students' writing should reflect an awareness that learning how to write is a process. Student writing should be evaluated on skills that have been taught in class or skills that have been previously learned. As more skills are taught, include them in the evaluation. Sharing scoring guides with students before they write—and sometimes giving them a voice in creating those checklists or rubrics—lets them know what is expected, guides them in their writing and revising, and gives them more of a sense of ownership of their writing. By looking at a rubric or guide used to score a finished piece of writing, students can see the level of success they have achieved in mastery of the skills taught for that assignment.

Part 1
Autobiographies

The autobiography places the writer in the center of the writing process, both subject and author. These six lessons encourage students to discover and express themselves by focusing on family heritage, pivotal personal experiences, or future projections.

Although Part 1 specifies the six activities of the writing process, it assumes students' previous experience with the process. If your class needs additional orientation, you will want to refer to lessons in *Writing 1: Learning the Process* to enrich their background. For example, if your students are unfamiliar with peer conferencing, or need a refresher course on how to offer constructive, diplomatic feedback to other writers, look at *Writing 1*, Lesson 10, "Conferencing: Putting Your Heads Together."

Note that you will need to allow sufficient drafting time between Lessons 2 and 4. Also, use of editing lessons varies depending on students' proficiency in grammar and usage. Let mechanics and usage needs reflected in student writing dictate which of these lessons to use and when. If the class needs more basic work in avoiding fragments and run-ons, substitute a review based on your grammar text for Lesson 5 ("Final Editing"). On the other hand, if students are ready for more advanced work, portions of editing lessons from later sections of this unit (Lessons 9, 15, 20, and 38) may be used.

In Part 1, students focus their efforts on a major writing assignment as they learn to compose and publish a well-developed autobiographical account. Although it may seem early in the writing program to include a major publishing effort, the activities in Lesson 6 ("Group Publishing Project") are incorporated to capitalize on students' natural interest in one another and to generate group enthusiasm for writing as a cooperative effort.

Lesson 1
Introducing Autobiographies

Objectives
- To recognize diverse approaches to autobiography
- To analyze the autobiographer's awareness of self, purpose, and audience

Notes to the Teacher
Autobiographers draw from an enormous body of knowledge—all of their previous life experiences—to compose stories of themselves. In selecting and arranging facts, events, and details, the writer both communicates and discovers self-concept.

In this lesson, students consider the opening paragraphs of autobiographies of some noteworthy Americans:

Diana Ross—former lead singer of the Motown group, the Supremes

Anthony Quinn—stage and screen star

Colin Powell—former National Security Advisor to President Bush and Chairman of the Joint Chiefs of Staff

Rose Kennedy—highly respected matriarch of the well-known Kennedy family

Louis Armstrong—famous jazz musician

Booker T. Washington—reformer, educator, author, former slave

Class discussion should provide an opportunity to assess students' awareness of the diverse approaches to autobiography.

Procedure
1. Write the word *autobiography* on the board, and ask students to define it (*a person's narration of the story of his or her life*).

2. Ask students to think about some real-life situations in which they might find themselves writing about significant events in their lives (*college and job applications, development of home pages, job "bios," family histories*).

3. Conduct a brief, open discussion based on these questions:
   - Have you ever read any autobiographies? Which ones? Why? Did you enjoy them?
   - Why would a person write an autobiography?
   - Why would a publisher publish a particular autobiography?

4. Have students complete **Handout 1**. Discuss responses.

Suggested Responses:

Secrets of a Sparrow
1. *with an important episode in her adulthood—a celebration of a playground she planned*
2. *creativity, children, her "roots"*
3. *expressive, energetic, talented, dreamer, lover of life*
4. *She will probably share the experiences and descriptions of the key people who helped shape her dreams.*

The Original Sin: A Self-Portrait
1. *Both start with adult experiences, but Quinn's emphasis is on disappointment while Diana Ross's is on success.*
2. *Quinn might go on to try to find true happiness.*
3. *Although Quinn has achieved outward success, he feels his life has been a failure.*

My American Journey
1. *Powell begins with near-death experience as an adult.*
2. *general readers who are familiar with his position in the military*
3. *He uses suspense, descriptive detail, dialogue; he will probably "tell a good story"*

Times to Remember
1. *perspective from old age*
2. *to form an integrated view of her life's terrors and tragedies: to emphasize "the good times"*
3. *reminiscences about specific experiences and people, especially family members*

3

My Life in New Orleans

1. *emphasis on the raucous, tumultuous neighborhood*

2. *"church people, gamblers, hustlers . . ."*

Up from Slavery

1. *at the very beginning—at his birth*

2. *He wants readers to know what it was like to be born into slavery and to rise out of it.*

3. *Booker T. Washington tells his story with objective solemnity. His matter-of-fact tone and his attempt to record detail accurately underline the appalling circumstances into which he was born—a world where men were treated as property.*

5. Ask students which autobiography they would choose to read, and why. Encourage students to discuss not only what they choose, but why. What is it about the author's style, approach, perspective, tone, etc. that appeals to them.

6. Point out that autobiographies can be diverse in the author's perspective, purpose and audience. When selecting from countless memories, authors make very different choices about what to tell and how to tell it.

   For instance, Diana Ross and Anthony Quinn chose to focus on very different types of formative events in their openers. Ross chose to describe an exhilarating experience (celebration of the opening of a park she designed in New York City) to emphasize a single, optimistic theme: success is open to all who work to attain their dreams. Quinn chose to describe the luncheon and to stress the negative realization he had—success does not mean a thing. Ross emphasizes a single optimistic theme, while Quinn ponders a negative psychological experience.

Colin Powell and Louis Armstrong use very different tones. Powell's approach is that of a dignified reporter, resulting in a somewhat distanced, but not impersonal, tone taken in describing a serious negative event. Armstrong's approach is vividly descriptive, resulting in the lively, conversational tone of a storyteller who is enjoying himself.

Quinn describes feelings that are very different from Rose Kennedy's. Ask students how they would characterize that difference. (*Quinn—confusion; Kennedy— serenity*).

Ross's language is very different from Powell's. Powell's straightforward, almost understated language, "I usually trust my instincts. This time I did not, which almost proved fatal," contrasts with Ross's exuberant conversational approach, "This was no normal state; it was a manifested figment of my imagination."

Ask students to share their observations.

7. Remind students that the next few lessons will lead them to write autobiographies. Suggest that they spend time thinking about possible approaches they might take to writing about their own life experiences. Allow them some class time to discuss some of these questions with a partner:

   • What general tone will you take?

   • What sort of language will you use?

   • For whom will you be writing?

   • With what key event(s) might you begin?

   • What "philosophy of life" might you convey?

   • What do you want the reader to know about you when they are finished?

A Sampling of Autobiographical Approaches

Directions: Autobiographies are as unique as the people who write them. They vary in style and purpose, as well as in starting point and prospective audience. The following excerpts open the autobiographies of six well-known Americans: Diana Ross, Anthony Quinn, Colin Powell, Rose Fitzgerald Kennedy, Louis Armstrong, and Booker T. Washington. Read each passage carefully and answer the questions that follow.

From *Secrets of a Sparrow*

At six P.M. on Thursday, July 21, 1983, the weather outside seemed completely calm, but inside my body, I was an electrical force bursting with energy. I wore a multicolored African robe. The opening of the show was to relate to my roots. Pictures of the African jungle were projected on a huge screen, interspersed with images of New York City, in itself another kind of jungle. I stood on the stairs adjacent to the huge platform stage. This was no normal stage; it was a manifested figment of my imagination. And I was about to step into a dream I had spent . . . a year conceiving and planning. Thousands of details. It had been grueling, like building a city from scratch. But what a city it was to be! A city of intensity and light. A city of creativity and vitality. A city that would eventually bring joy to the children. I'm a dreamer. And that's what I did in Central Park. I picked a dream, a goal, and then imagined all the details, drew it up like a blueprint, designed it, and then I knew it would happen. I believe that existence is magical, that we can think of something and bring it into being. . . . [And] build it I did. A playground on West Eighty-first Street in Central Park. There are few people who know, but that's not important. What does matter is that as you read this, children are having fun and running and laughing and safely playing with each other. . . .[1]

1. Where does Diana Ross begin?

2. What does she seem to value?

3. What is your impression of Diana Ross, based on this excerpt?

4. What sorts of incidents do you expect to find in the rest of this autobiography?

[1]Diana Ross, *Secrets of a Sparrow* (New York: Villard Books, 1993), 3–4, 12.

From *The Original Sin: A Self Portrait*

I was living in New York, surrounded by possessions, family and position. I had three pictures running simultaneously on Times Square and I was appearing in a play at the same time. Everywhere you looked on Broadway you saw my name in lights.

Some lovely ladies from a drama society gave a luncheon for me. They invited prominent personalities from many fields to pay me homage.

When I was called upon, I tried to thank them. I started haltingly. I looked out at the sea of friendly faces before me, waiting expectantly. Then I heard myself mumbling that I felt like a total failure. I can still recall the shock and dismay that greeted my words. Everyone wanted a light, gracious talk and there I stood declaring that success to me did not mean a thing.[2]

1. How does Anthony Quinn's approach differ from Diana Ross's in starting point and emphasis?

2. What impressions do you receive from this opening? What do you predict?

3. What irony seems to underlie this autobiography?

[2]Anthony Quinn, *The Original Sin: A Self-Portrait* (Boston: Little Brown and Company, 1972), 3.

From *My American Journey*

The day was pure Jamaica in February, the sun brilliant overhead, the air soft with only the hint of an afternoon thundershower. Perfect flying weather, as we boarded the UH-I helicopter. My wife, Alma, and I were visiting the island of my parents' birth at the invitation of Prime Minister Michael Manley. Manley had been after me for a year, ever since the Gulf War. "Get some rest, dear boy," he had said in that compelling lilt the last time he had called. "Come home, if only for a few days. Stay at our government guesthouse." This time I accepted with pleasure.[3]

1. How does Colin Powell's starting point differ from both Diana Ross's and Anthony Quinn's?

2. What kind of audience does Powell seem to anticipate?

3. What does his opening suggest about the style in which Powell's life story will be told?

[3]Colin Powell with Joseph Persico, *My American Journey* (New York: Random House, 1995), 3.

From *Times to Remember*

There have been times when I felt I was one of the more fortunate people in the world, almost as if Providence, or Fate, or Destiny, as you like, had chosen me for special favors.

Now I am in my eighties, and I have known the joys and sorrows of a full life. I can neither forget nor ever reconcile myself to the tragedies. Age, however, has its privileges. One is to reminisce and another is to reminisce selectively. I prefer to remember the good times, and that is how this book begins.[4]

1. Rose Kennedy tells her story from a different point in life than the other autobiographers. How does her perspective differ from theirs?

2. What is Rose Kennedy's central purpose in writing her autobiography?

3. What do you predict you would find if you read her autobiography in its entirety?

[4]Rose Fitzgerald Kennedy, *Times to Remember* (Garden City, N.Y.: Doubleday & Co., Inc., 1974), 1.

From *Satchmo: My Life in New Orleans*

When I was born in 1900 my father, Willie Armstrong, and my mother, May Ann—or Mayann as she was called—were living on a little street called James Alley. Only one block long, James Alley is located in the crowded section of New Orleans known as Back o' Town. It is one of the four great sections into which the city is divided. The others are Uptown, Downtown and Front o' Town, and each of these quarters has its own little traits.

James Alley—not Jane Alley as some people call it—lies in the very heart of what is called The Battlefield because the toughest characters in town used to live there, and would shoot and fight so much. In that one block between Gravier and Perdido Streets more people were crowded than you ever saw in your life. There were churchpeople, gamblers, hustlers, cheap pimps, thieves, prostitutes and lots of children. There were bars, honky-tonks and saloons, and lots of women walking the streets for tricks to take to their "pads," as they called their rooms.

Mayann told me that the night I was born there was a great big shooting scrape in the Alley and the two guys killed each other. It was the Fourth of July, a big holiday in New Orleans, when almost anything can happen. Pretty near everybody celebrates with pistols, shot guns, or any other weapon that's handy.[5]

1. What does Louis Armstrong describe in the opening of his autobiography—in contrast with the other four autobiographers?

2. What specific colorful details does Armstrong incorporate?

[5]Louis Armstrong, *Satchmo: My Life in New Orleans* (Englewood Cliffs, N.J.: Prentice-Hall, Inc., 1954), 7–8.

From *Up from Slavery*

I was born a slave on a plantation in Franklin County, Virginia. I am not quite sure of the exact place or exact date of my birth, but at any rate I suspect I must have been born somewhere and at some time. As nearly as I have been able to learn, I was born near a cross-roads post-office called Hale's Ford, and the year was 1858 or 1859. I do not know the month or the day. The earliest impressions I can now recall are of the plantation and the slave quarters—the latter being the part of the plantation where the slaves had their cabins.

My life had its beginning in the midst of the most miserable, desolate, and discouraging surroundings. This was so, however, not because my owners were especially cruel, for they were not, as compared with many others. I was born in a typical log cabin, about fourteen by sixteen feet square. In this cabin I lived with my mother and a brother and sister till after the Civil War, when we were all declared free.[6]

1. At what point in Booker T. Washington's life does he begin his autobiography?

2. What does Washington's purpose seem to be in telling his life story?

3. What is the language and tone of these opening paragraphs—in contrast with the other five selections?

---

[6]Booker T. Washington, *Up From Slavery* (1901; reprint, with an introduction by William L. Andrews, New York: Oxford University Press, 1995), 1.

Lesson 2
Autobiographical Approaches

Objectives
* To recognize three approaches to autobiographical writing
* To generate ideas for autobiographies

Notes to the Teacher
Because students enjoy sharing their experiences, autobiographical essays generate high student interest. Composing the autobiography is a challenge because of the difficulty in examining one's life objectively. Adding to that difficulty is the need to select from the broad spectrum of each person's experience.

To help focus students' self-examination, **Handout 2** presents three autobiographical approaches: family autobiography, significant event autobiography, and futurography. A brainstorming activity helps students generate ideas for their essays.

In the family history portion of the lesson, be sensitive to the fact that many students may have alternative family structures—blended families, adoptive parents, single-parent families, etc.

Procedure
1. Read students the titles of some best-selling autobiographies. Ask, "Why have these very different people all chosen to write their autobiographies?" Remind students that people write autobiographies for diverse reasons.

2. Point out that autobiographies are necessarily selective because no one can write about everything that has happened to him or her.

3. Identify three autobiographical approaches—family autobiography, significant event autobiography, and futurography—and write these terms on the board.

4. Have students speculate about what a family autobiography is. Read aloud an excerpt from one. (Two good examples are *America, America* by Elia Kazan and *Roots* by Alex Haley.) Point out that this approach involves exploration of the history of the family rather than a focus on the individual.

5. Tell students that Anglo-Saxon last names have four major sources: occupation (Smith); patronym (Fitzpatrick); location (Hill); description (Longfellow). Ask students what they know about derivations of other types of last names from around the world.

6. Have students complete part A of **Handout 2**. (Students will probably need to consult some name books and talk with their families before finishing this section.) As an extension of this activity, have students orally research their parents' or guardians' lives and trace their family trees. Encourage them to use any available family tree-making software for gathering and recording this information. Either give students free rein to trace as far back as they want, or else direct them to stop after a selected number of generations.

7. Have students speculate about what a significant event autobiography is. Read an excerpt from a model (such as *Black Boy* by Richard Wright or *100 Years, 100 Stories* by George Burns) and inform students that this type of autobiography often recounts important moments when people realize something new about themselves. Examples: falling in or out of love; acquiring a friend; the death of someone close to them; a valued accomplishment; learning something that changes your philosophy of life. Have the class brainstorm more examples as you write them on the board.

8. Have students freewrite part B of **Handout 2**. Emphasize generation of ideas instead of precision. Have volunteers read from their handouts.

9. Have students speculate about what the third type of autobiography—the futurography—is. Inform students that, as the name suggests, this type of writing involves prediction about what the person's future holds. Discuss how dreams and goals shape us as much as our past experiences. Tell students to project themselves twenty years into the future. Have them complete part C and share responses.

10. Direct students to choose one of the autobiographical forms and write first drafts of their autobiographies, with their classmates as the target audience. (For students who need it, demonstrate a prewriting graphic organizer such as a timeline or web.) Suggest an approximate length and set an appropriate deadline. Remind students to specify on their drafts which of the three forms of autobiography they have chosen.

Types of Autobiography

Part A.

Directions: A *family autobiography* is your story within the framework of your heritage. Answer the following questions. Let your ideas flow and do not worry at this point about being entirely accurate or precise.

1. What does your first name mean?

2. What is the origin of your last name?

3. How and where did your parents meet?

4. How and why did one of your ancestors come to live in this area?

5. How has a family experience that occurred before you were born affected your life?

Part B.

Directions: A *significant event autobiography* is the story of key events in your life. Answer the following questions. Let your ideas flow and do not worry at this point about being entirely accurate or precise.

1. What are three events in your life that had a big impact on you?

    a.

    b.

    c.

2. Select one of the three events above to examine in more detail.

    a. When and where did the event occur?

    b. Who was involved?

    c. What took place?

    d. How did the individuals involved react?

    e. What other details do you remember about the individuals and the situation?

    f. What do you remember about exactly what was said during the event?

    g. How did the event change you?

Part C.

Directions: A *futurography* is a story projecting into your future; fiction based on present facts, values, hopes, and dreams. Answer the following questions to explore what you think your future holds.

1. What year is it?

2. Where do you live?

3. What type of home do you have? What is the neighborhood like?

4. What is your marital status?

5. Describe your appearance and health.

6. Do you have any children? If so, what are their names and ages?

7. Describe your friends.

8. What kind of job do you have? What do you do when you are not at work?

9. What is your annual income?

10. What is the biggest problem you face?

11. List some of your noteworthy accomplishments.

12. Describe your special interests and hobbies.

13. Do you have any other future goals?

Lesson 3
Student Response Sampler

Objective
• To provide a model for peer response papers

Notes to the Teacher
With guidance from the teacher, students can help their peers by responding to each other's papers. Having written an autobiography with the class as a target audience, each student will now share some aspect of his or her life with the group. It is essential that such sharing takes place within a safe, supportive environment. To ensure that such an environment of mutual respect exists, review and model for students how to make positive comments on others' papers while asking clarifying questions and offering respectful, constructive criticism. Use what you have observed in classroom interactions to decide how students will be grouped for peer conferencing. Finally, make it clear that no verbal hostility will be tolerated.

To assess students' ability to provide constructive, courteous criticism to their peers, lead a class exercise in which they respond to an anonymous paper from another class. Model for students how to comment on strengths—areas where the writing is rich in content or well-organized—while making helpful suggestions for improving the paper, such as ideas about where to add more supportive detail or where to eliminate redundancy. The focus should not, at this point, be on mechanical errors, which can be corrected later, during the editing process.

Procedure
1. Have students read the selection on **Handout 3** silently and jot down responses to the questions that follow it.

2. Ask the following questions:
   a. What is the writer's purpose? What is his point in telling us about this particular game?
   b. Who is the writer's audience? Do you think you have to be a basketball fan to appreciate this piece?
   c. What actions does the writer describe as part of his experience?
   d. Who is involved in this story?
   e. How do the other individuals react to the central figure?
   f. Are the main idea and supporting ideas presented in a way that makes sense to you?
   g. What part of this paper do you like best?
   h. Is there anything in this piece that you do not understand? What?
   i. Is Dennis a hero in any sense of the word? Why or why not?
   j. To which of your emotions does the writer appeal? How?

3. Tell students to focus for a time on the content and plan of the paper rather than on mechanical errors. Mistakes in spelling, punctuation, and capitalization can be corrected in the editing process, which comes later.

4. Divide the class into groups of four. Have them complete **Handout 4** independently, then discuss their answers.

   Suggested Responses:
   1. *to share a difficult moment that led her to decide on a new purpose in life*
   2. *obtaining Old Shep; the dog's death*
   3. *father and other adults—caring; sister— teasing*
   4. *Most students will agree that the sequencing and connections are clear.*
   6. *The story is a series of flashbacks. The writer starts by going back to the night after Old Shep died, goes farther back to the day the writer got Old Shep, moves on to the writer's life with Shep, continues up to the evening Old Shep died, and ends where the piece began—the night after Old Shep died.*
   7. *The use of flashback lends the story immediacy and power; the writer allows the reader into her head and the reader gets to follow the actual train of thought and memory.*

5. Remind students to bring first drafts of their autobiographies to the next class.

17

Discussing a Student Paper

Directions: Read the following piece about the writer's memory of one particularly fateful basketball game, and complete the five statements. Be prepared you for class discussion of this piece of writing.

My Time on the Line

I hope all of you have the chance to be a hero. Then we'll compare notes. Mine came last year on the junior varsity basketball team. Through hours of daily practice, and from my blood lineage to the coach (he's my uncle), I had made the team as the thirteenth man on a twelve-man squad. I could do many things well—run, jump, rebound, and especially foul people—but I could rarely put that ball through the hoop.

That's why Uncle Bob (or, in public, "Mr. Chambers") would only put me in when we were winning by thirty points, with one minute to go. One game I was even credited with scoring two points off a rebound, although the ball really bounced off the opposing guy's hands.

My dad went to every game. I liked it but I didn't. His hair seemed to get grayer as he watched me sit on the bench.

"Dad," I'd tell him, "save your money and just watch me in a living room chair." He said he enjoyed the games and that he was proud of me, although compared to my older brother, who once was all-conference, I didn't see how.

Actually, I enjoyed the bench. My best friend, George Coughlin, also never played, so we had a good time dreaming of games we'd win with fifty-foot swishes.

And then the fun and dreams ended. I had to play in a meaningful game.

On the third to last game of the season, against John Marshall, when we were still tied for first place, four of our players, including two starters, got the flu and couldn't play. That left eight of us, and you can bet both Uncle Bob and I were getting nervous about my contributions. I prayed that the game would immediately get out of hand, that we'd be winning by fifty points at halftime and the other team would go home. As it happened, the game was tied with two minutes to go in the first half. With Kelly Donnelly twisting his ankle, Uncle Bob glumly told me to check in.

In two minutes I succeeded in missing two shots, fouling once, and watching the ball sail through my fingers.

My Dad looked older every minute. I think he wanted to put a bag on his head. So did I.

In the third quarter, our guard, Jimmy Chamberlain, got hot and helped build up a ten-point lead by the fourth quarter. I was breathing easier until Jimmy got in a fight with a player from John Marshall and both were ejected. I started praying the roof would collapse and we all could go home.

With all our injuries, and with the importance of this game, the crowd started getting thunderous. Without Jimmy Chamberlain, however, even this rabid crowd support could not help us; our lead chipped away. With two minutes left, and our team ahead by a scant two points, the horrendous happened.

Rick Mays fouled out.

Uncle Bob would have preferred to stay with four players, but that was technically impossible. So with all the confidence in the world, he turned to me and implored, "Dennis, try not to foul."

With the crowd screaming and clapping and jumping in the stands, I felt totally displaced, as though I were a gladiator in the Roman Coliseum. The blood seemed to have been cut off from my wobbly legs, and puddles of sweat formed on my palms. I had never been so close to the scoreboard. Its red and green lights looked pretty, just like a Christmas tree.

"Jason, cover number 38!" Uncle Bob screamed.

Oh no, last name meant trouble. Number 38, a thin kid with floppy blond hair, the kid I should have been covering, was wide open under the basket. He made the shot, and I lunged for and fouled him. He made the foul shot.

I thought I saw my Dad crawl under the stands. Uncle Bob was pointing at me, but I couldn't hear him, nor could I hear the crowd. However, I could feel the floor shake when we sank the next shot. I ran back to cover number 38. His skin felt like a wet seal's. He didn't seem like such a bad guy, although as my opponent, he was supposed to arouse some sort of loathing in me. He got the ball. I slapped it away (a hero for five seconds), we failed to score, and, with twenty seconds left, they made a long jumper.

Uncle Bob called time out. We were down by one point. I stood in the circle while Uncle Bob diagrammed a play for Ben Breiner. I looked up to see kids and grownups howling like wolves. I also saw Laurie Anderson, the girl whose image had been tormenting me daily. I think she saw me. If Ben Breiner made this shot, I'd be their hero. And hers.

"Jason," Uncle Bob screamed, "do you understand?"

I understood. Ben Breiner had to make the shot. The clock started ticking, players started scrambling, my heart started racing, and the rafters started banging. Ben Breiner took a shot from the baseline. I watched the ball arch toward the basket, carom off the rim, and fall into my hands. Like a live grenade, I tried to throw it back to Ben, but number 38, whom now I did loathe, fouled me.

The referee mistakenly thought I was trying to shoot the ball, so with three seconds to go I approached the foul line to attempt two shots. The opposing coach ranted and called a time out. In the team huddle, my teammates slapped my back and said I could do it. Uncle Bob told me to relax, for I only had to make one shot.

But two shots and I'd be a hero. Two shots and the school would hoist me on its shoulder and carry me around like a pharaoh. Two shots and Laurie Anderson would take my hand and stroll with me under the full moon. Two shots and life would be a whole lot better.

I had practiced so hard at foul shots, but I could never do better than 33%. At the foul line, the basket looked like a small pea at the small end of a telescope.

All dimensions seemed to warp. My fingertips throbbed and sprinkled sweat. The weight of the world pressed against my shoulder. The hopes and expectations of the entire world.

I looked at the bench with longing and aching.

I aimed at the rim, bounced the ball four times, and released it. The ball cracked against the rim and fired itself back at my feet. The crowd groaned and number 38 snickered.

I hoped some assassin might take aim. Just a flesh wound, but still I'd be a hero.

The referee handed me the ball. My saturated fingers could barely grip it. The basket, the floor, the gym seemed to tremble. If I were brave, I would have screamed and hurled that ball into the stands. Instead, I bounced the ball once and shot it. The ball lazily floated toward the basket, hit the back of the rim, and like a geyser, shot up high and over the backboard.

On the incoming pass, we deliberately fouled number 38. He made both shots and we lost 57–54.

That year we finished in second place.

My father, as he did after every game, drove me home. I had suppressed my tears in the locker room, but now, in the dark of our car, they burst out. I cried and babbled that I stunk and that I was quitting basketball.

I was ashamed I had lost the game. Randy, my brother, never lost a game.

My father let me cry. As we pulled into the garage he placed his hand on my shoulder. "Dennis, you have nothing to be ashamed about. You played your best and I'm proud of you, Son. I'm just as proud of you as I was of Randy. It was just a game, Dennis. The important thing is not winning basketball games but treating people well. I'm proud of the way you're growing up, Dennis."

That's what I remember him saying, and it made me feel a lot better. I took the game less seriously, and strangely my basketball skills improved. I'm on the varsity team, again as the thirteenth man on a twelve-man squad, but this time the coach isn't my uncle. I still don't play much, but I have a lot of fun because my teammates are great guys.

And perhaps someday, with the game on the line, I'll even make those foul shots.

—Dennis Jason

1. Jason's piece is about _____

   _____ .

2. Jason's main point is that he learned _____

   _____ .

3. As I "listen" to this piece, I imagine the writer's tone of voice to be _____ and

   that he is writing for an audience made up of _____ .

4. One sentence in this piece that I wish I had written is: _____

   _____ .

5. One question I have for the writer before he writes another draft is:_____

   _____ .

Becoming a Peer Critic

Directions: Read the following piece about the writer's memory of a loss. As you read, note the draft's strengths and its weaknesses. Then respond to the writing by answering the questions.

Legacy of Loyalty

The night Old Shep died, Dad came into my room, sat on the edge of the bed, leaned towards me and opened his mouth. No words came out though. I guessed that he wanted to have a father-daughter talk about death, but couldn't manage it. Poor dad! I couldn't help him either. My insides were as hard and cracked as a dried-out river bed. I just lay there without moving. I could hear my clock ticking away the minutes 'til midnight struck on the town clock. About a minute after midnight, Dad got up without a word and went to his room. I heard the door close quietly. I wondered if he was pacing the floor. Dad paced when he was upset. I lay there for about ten more minutes: the next thing I knew it was morning. The sun was shining through the curtains, but I had a hard time getting up. The lump in my chest had grown to the size of a cannonball. I remember wondering how Dad was, and then I thought of Old Shep out there in the orchard where we had buried him, and the cannonball plowed a path through my heart.

I can still remember the day Dad announced at the supper table he was taking me to the mall after we finished eating. It was my ninth birthday and Dad had promised me my very own pup. When Kitty heard Dad and I were going to Puppy World, she set up a fierce howl. "I want to go too, Mom can I too?" Dad gave Mom a wink, and she said to Kitty in her stern voice (reserved for "special" occasions), "You'll stay home with me, Kitty, and help with the dishes." Kitty started to whine and called me "the most selfish sister anyone every had," but Mom glared at her and sent her to get small plates for the cake. I could hardly eat even one piece of my favorite cake—chocolate with cream cheese icing—I was so excited. Usually I have no trouble downing at least two pieces.

Finally, dinner was over and Kitty began clearing the table. As she passed me, she whispered loudly in my ear, "Selfish." Dad was going down the hall already jingling the car keys, and I dashed after him without a backward glance at poor Kitty.

At Puppy World the pups were in small cages along one wall, and I got kind of sick when I saw them. They had hardly any room to turn around in. Dad and I looked at them all without speaking. Then he said, "Kelly, do you like the golden retriever?" I sure did, but my eyes were glued to a sad-eyed collie with a long muzzle. I just knew he had to be mine.

"Dad, I want that one," I whispered, pointing to the collie, "and I'm going to call him Old Shep." I could see Dad smile a little when he heard that name, but he didn't say anything. Dad never commented when you said or did anything people thought was stupid. He was like that. He just smiled a little and never said anything to hurt you. Not like Kitty. When you did anything she didn't like, she screamed. "Oh, how stupid can you get" and held her head between her hands. I knew that when we got home and Dad introduced the puppy to the family and told them his name was Old Shep, Kitty would have one of her fits.

Sure enough, what I had predicted happened. When Kitty heard the name Old Shep she shrieked, "Ha, you don't have *any* imagination." I didn't pay a bit of attention to her. I knew she was suffering from a bad case of jealousy, and just in case it was catching, I went outside under the oak tree with Old Shep. He snuggled up close to me because it was getting a little chilly.

Well, that was five years ago. Old Shep had been a faithful companion on my journey through middle school and junior high. He went with me everywhere—to the school bus in the morning, on bike rides to the lake in the summer.

Bike rides! For days after Old Shep died I couldn't even look at my bike lying behind the old car Dad was overhauling. I had used it last that painful evening.

It was dusk, my favorite time when the deepening darkness transformed the countryside and spread a blanket of peace on fields and road. I decided to ride my bike to Peggy Butler's house to see her new video game. Naturally, as soon as I got my bike out Old Shep was at my side. I whizzed down McNeil's Hill with the wind whistling past and Old Shep running alongside on the left. Just as I was about to make the sharp turn at the bottom, I heard a car coming from the rear at a terrific speed.

The next thing I knew I was down a slight incline whole and sound, and so was my bike. But Old Shep was lying in the road, a mangled heap of torn flesh and broken bones. He had steered me into the ditch, taking the full impact of the speeding car.

I lay on the road, sobbing, and cradling and comforting Old Shep. I had to get help but I couldn't move. Fortunately our next-door neighbor, Mr. Powell, was driving home on the other side. He saw us in the brightness of his headlights, stopped and sized up the situation right away. He got an old blanket from the trunk, and together we lifted Old Shep on it as gently as we could. By the time we got to the vet, I knew it was all over for the dog who had saved my life. Doc Leland did all he could.

An hour later I heard the police had caught the drunken speeder. The time that had passed since I started for Peggy's house had been a nightmare, but one good thing—no, two things—had happened.

For some strange reason, Kitty never called me stupid or selfish again. But better than that, I had decided what I was going to do with my life. I was going to imitate Old Shep. That night as I lay awake with Dad sitting on my bed not saying a word, I made up my mind to give my life to save others' lives. I didn't know then exactly how I'd do it. I had plenty of time yet to decide whether I'd be a researcher, a doctor, a firefighter or . . .

1. What is the writer's purpose in writing about these particular events?

2. What are the key incidents recounted in this autobiographical piece?

3. How do the other individuals react to the central figure in the piece?

4. Does the story make sense to you? Which part do you like best?

5. Is any part confusing to you? Why?

6. How is the story organized in contrast with the actual timing of events?

7. How does the way the story is organized enhance its impact?

Lesson 4
Strategy for Group Conferencing

Objective

• To practice peer response strategies

Notes to the Teacher

The previous lesson provided the experience of responding to an unknown student's paper. In this lesson, students will respond to their classmates' first drafts. Remind them that the process is the same: read, respect, and recommend helpful suggestions for improvement. While students are discussing papers, move from group to group, listening, commenting, responding to questions, and assessing their ability to respond helpfully and respectfully to one another's papers.

Procedure

1. Divide the class in pairs according to the type of autobiography they chose in Lesson 2. Provide as much space between pairs as possible. Be sure each student has a first draft paper.

2. Distribute **Handout 5**.

3. Tell students to exchange first drafts. Have them write both their names and their partners' names on each response sheet.

4. Instruct students to read their partner's paper silently and jot down their initial reactions on the response sheet.

5. Have partners take turns sharing responses and discussing ways of improving the papers.

6. Assign the writing of a second draft. Remind students to consider their classmates' suggestions; they may choose to accept and incorporate some ideas and reject others.

7. After the second draft is written, have students staple it on top of the first draft and the peer response sheet, so that they have an ongoing record of the transformations the essay undergoes.

8. At the next session, divide the class into groups of four; students who were originally partners should now be in different groups. Distribute another copy of **Handout 5**. Remind students to have their stapled packet (both drafts plus first response sheet) with them.

9. Tell students that professional writers usually have several people read their manuscripts in order to get as many helpful reactions and suggestions as possible before the manuscript goes to the printer. Some drafts go through several revisions.

10. Direct the students to read their own second drafts aloud to the group. Each group member should listen carefully and then respond orally to the questions on **Handout 5**. Authors may clarify their points of view if they feel that someone misunderstood what they were trying to say. Authors should also note on the response sheet any peer comments that might be helpful during the next revision.

11. Direct students to complete new (third) drafts of their papers for the next class. Tell them that they will then do final editing (correction of any errors in spelling, punctuation, grammar, or usage) before turning in a final copy to you.

Writer's Exchange

Directions: Exchange papers with your partner and read your partner's paper silently. Circle which of the three autobiographical approaches the writer has chosen. Then respond to the paper by writing your answers to the appropriate questions below.

Partner's Name_____

Autobiographical approach   a. family history   b. significant event   c. futurography

1. Does the writer keep the focus sharp and clear?

    a. Are all the details about the family setting?

    b. Are all the details about the significant event that changed him or her in some way?

    c. Are all the details about his or her projected future?

    If there are any details that you feel may not be relevant to the writer's focus, list them.

2. Does the writer support each general statement with enough specific detail? If you think this area needs work, list general statements that you feel could use more detailed explanations or more concrete examples.

3. Select at least three examples of the writer's good word choices and list them below. (These might include precise nouns, vivid verbs, colorful phrases, etc.)

4. Which of the writer's recollections (or predictions) do you find most interesting?

5. Is there something missing—something you expected to hear, but did not? What?

6. Is it clear to you why the writer chose these particular events to share? Explain.

7. What do you "see" as you read this piece? Is there something you would like the writer to help you visualize—or hear, or smell, or taste, or feel—more clearly?

8. How has the writer organized the events in this piece? Are they arranged in chronological order (as they happened, or will happen)? Does the writer use flashback?

    Would changing the order of events improve this piece? How?

Lesson 5
Final Editing

Objectives
- To correct common spelling errors, use proper agreement, and generate a variety of sentence structures
- To edit drafts, specifically in the areas of spelling, agreement, and sentence structure

Notes to the Teacher

Many students equate writing a good essay with writing one that is mechanically correct. While proper mechanics are essential for clarity, they have sometimes been emphasized at inappropriate stages of the writing process, often with the result of impeding students' creativity. The editing activity should come after drafting and revising, so that students can first concentrate on expressing and organizing ideas before focusing on grammar, usage, and mechanics. The handout in this lesson allows for assessment of students' ability to correct common spelling errors, use proper agreement, and vary sentence structures.

Use this and all subsequent editing lessons at your discretion based on students' editing needs. This lesson discusses spelling, agreement, and sentence structure and can be supplemented by any good English handbook. Some suggestions are

The Handbook of Good English. Edward D. Johnson. New York: Facts on File, 1991.

The Least You Should Know about English: Writing Skills. Teresa F. Glazier. Fort Worth: Harcourt Brace College Publishers, 1997.

Writers INC. Patrick Sebranek, et al. Wilmington, Mass.: Great Source Education Group, Inc., 1995.

Write Source 2000: A Guide to Writing, Thinking, and Learning. Patrick Sebranek, et al. Wilmington, Mass.: Great Source Education Group, Inc., 1995.

Procedure
1. Discuss students' personal attitudes toward the study of grammar. What do students think that teachers mean when they talk about studying grammar? Why is it taught? Should it be? How have students enjoyed past grammar study and exercises they have done? Did they find some ways of learning about grammar and usage more effective and more enjoyable than others?

2. Discuss the necessity of rules. What would happen if there were no out-of-bounds in sports? no traffic rules? no rules about what behavior is and is not allowed in public? no rules about acceptable written and spoken classroom language? Lead students to understand that we have grammatical rules not just for the sake of having rules, but to make communication more clear. For example, the listener in the following situation may not understand what is meant by the speaker who disregards a certain rule about ambiguous pronouns: "Erin met Tanya in the hall, and they went back to her desk."

3. Write the word *ghoti* on the board and ask students to pronounce it. Explain that George Bernard Shaw's answer would be *fish* and ask students if they can figure out why. If necessary, explain that English spelling is not uniformly phonetic; there are few hard-and-fast spelling rules. Thus, a person adhering to three rules that sometimes work—*gh* pronounced *f* as in *cough*; *o* pronounced *i* as in *women*; and *ti* pronounced *sh* as in *nation*—would pronounce *ghoti* as *fish*.

4. For other examples of how irregular spelling and pronunciation can be, ask students for words that illustrate different ways to pronounce *ough* (*cough, rough, bough, through,* and *thorough*).

5. Emphasize that having difficulty spelling is not a sign of stupidity. The "proper" way to spell a particular word often seems to have no rhyme or reason. Students might enjoy "A Plan for the Improvement of English Spelling," a humorous piece by Mark Twain that makes this point. The piece is reprinted in the September 1999 issue of *Literary Cavalcade.* Back issues can be obtained by writing to

Literary Cavalcade
Scholastic, Inc.
555 Broadway
New York, NY 10012-3999

6. Point out that, on the other hand, many readers think less of a piece of writing that contains careless spelling errors. Fortunately,

there are several common mistakes that anyone can learn to avoid—and there are now spell checkers in word processing programs that can help a writer quickly identify and correct many spelling errors.

7. Review the differences between *its* and *it's*; *affect* and *effect*; *who's* and *whose*; *your* and *you're*; *they're*, *their*, and *there*.

Point out that using the wrong word in one of these pairs or groups is a spelling error that a spell checker will not catch. A hilarious essay by Dave Barry, "Monkey with a Word Processor," emphasizes this. This piece is also reprinted in the September 1999 issue of *Literary Cavalcade*.

Have students generate short sentences that use each troublesome word correctly and share these orally as you write them on the board. You could then place these on large cards to be posted on the wall as visual reminders.

8. Have students read part A of **Handout 6** and complete the exercise. Discuss the answers.

   Suggested Responses:

   1. *it's, its*
   2. *effect, affect*
   3. *Whose, Who's*
   4. *you're, your*
   5. *they're, there, their*

As an extension, you may want to go over a longer list of frequently confused word pairs and triplets. Such lists can be found in most English handbooks.

9. Have students complete part B of the handout. Review the answers and the rules. Encourage students to put these rules in "regular English"—and supply some simple examples—as if they were explaining them to a friend. For example, to explain rule 8, you might say, "Sometimes when writing a sentence, you have a subject like *economics* or *two weeks* and you have to decide whether to use a singular verb like *is* or a plural one like *are*. Just ask yourself whether you would replace the subject with *it* or *they*. Economics __ my favorite subject. *It is* my favorite subject. Two weeks __ a long time to wait. *It is* a long time to wait. Subjects that end in "s" don't always take plural verbs!"

Suggested Responses:

1. *dislikes—A singular subject requires a singular verb.*

2. *go—A plural subject requires a plural verb.*

3. *is—Compound subjects joined by and and considered as one unit require a singular verb.*

4. *are—Compound subjects joined by and and considered as two or more units require a plural verb.*

5. *is—Verbs for compound subjects joined by or or nor agree with the subject closer to them.*

6. *are—Same as preceding rule*

7. *knows—Certain words are plural in meaning, but are grammatically singular and require a singular verb; i.e.,* everyone, anyone, no one, everybody, anybody, nobody, every, any.

8. *is—Certain words are plural in form, but singular in meaning; these require a singular verb: i.e.,* civics, athletics, economics, fifty dollars, statistics, two weeks.

9. *he—A pronoun must agree with its antecedent in gender and number.*

10. *his or her—Indefinite pronouns are singular in form and require a singular verb and a singular pronoun.*

11. *her—same as preceding rule*

12. *its—A collective noun considered as a single unit requires a singular verb.*

13. *their—If the members of a group are considered individually, the pronoun referring to them is plural.*

14. *themselves—Pronouns must agree with their antecedents in person.*

10. Use part C of the handout to review the four structural types of sentences. Allow volunteers to share the sentences of each type that they have created.

11. Have students apply what they have learned as they edit their own drafts in part D.

12. Direct students to complete their final autobiography drafts. **Handout 7,** an evaluation rubric, can be used to guide and assess these final drafts.

Editing Guidelines

Part A.

Directions: Read the following information before completing the sentences with the correct form of the word.

Many words in English are hard to spell. Do not be overly concerned with spelling when you are writing your first draft. Use the words that best communicate your ideas, and spell them the best you can. During the editing stage, however, correct spelling becomes necessary so that your audience can follow your ideas—and can appreciate that you have taken the time to polish your work.

To improve your spelling:

a. Keep a notebook of troublesome words.

b. Memorize the most commonly misspelled words in the English language. Memorize them now, and you will not have to refer to the dictionary later.

c. Try one of these methods:

  • Use your finger and trace the word on your palm or arm.

  • Close your eyes and visualize the word.

  • On a piece of paper, design the word, giving special attention to any troublesome letters.

  • Use a word's letters as lyrics of a song you know.

  • Skim your composition backward, word by word, letting your eyes scan for words that do not look right.

d. Always have a dictionary or your word notebook nearby.

1. (its, it's) I know that _____ hard to believe, but the idea has lost _____ appeal already.

2. (affect, effect) The new law goes into _____ soon. I wonder how it will _____ us.

3. (Whose, Who's) The coach asked, "_____ socks are these? _____ going to claim them?"

4. (your, you're) If _____ going to the mall, you had better take _____ wallet.

5. (there, their, they're) I think _____ over _____ in _____ mother's car.

Part B.

Directions: Audiences for your writing—such as teachers, admissions committees, and potential employers—do tend to notice grammatical errors and form negative impressions of writers who make them. Subject-verb and pronoun-antecedent agreement allows your audience to understand your writing and not be distracted by errors in form. Underline the correct word in each of the following sentences.

1. Pedro (dislike, dislikes) football games when there is an overpowering team.

2. The men (go, goes) home at the end of each week.

3. Spaghetti and meatballs (is, are) a very tasty meal.

4. Leah and Stacey (is, are) swimming daily.

5. Jordan or Natalie (is, are) going to be the next class president.

6. Jamie or the twins (is, are) vacationing in Mexico.

7. Everyone (know, knows) the right format for writing a composition.

8. The mumps (is, are) a miserable disease that most children today never get.

9. Ryan had gone to the library before (he, they) was missed.

10. Everybody has to do (his or her, their) job in order for the work to get done.

11. Neither of the girls has done (her, their) homework.

12. The family had just returned from (its, their) annual summer vacation.

13. After deliberation, the jury tallied (its, their) votes.

14. She said to the preschoolers, "Children should clean up after (themselves, yourselves)."

Part C.

Directions: Read the following information and create your own sentences.

Most of us like variety—in our clothes, our food, and our experiences. Imagine that you ate your favorite food for every meal. It would soon stop being your favorite food. The same applies to writing. Varying your sentences makes your writing more interesting and effective.

English has a number of sentence structures to communicate your thoughts. The more familiar you become with these structures, the easier it will be for you to include a variety of them in your writing—and to use the structure that best fits your meaning.

There are four basic types of sentence structures: simple sentences, compound sentences, complex sentences, and compound-complex sentences.

1. Here are two simple sentences:
   Snow is falling.
   In the middle of the night, the fire engine raced to the burning building.

   A simple sentence contains one independent clause (a complete idea that could stand alone as a sentence) and no subordinate clauses (ideas with subjects and verbs that could not stand alone).

   Write your own example of a simple sentence.

2. Here are two compound sentences:
   I whistled to my dog, and he ran toward me.
   The day was warm, but many students wore sweaters.

   A compound sentence contains two or more independent clauses (complete ideas joined by words like *and, or,* or *but*).

   Write your own example of a compound sentence.

3. Here are two complex sentences:
   When no one was looking, I sneaked into the room.
   He is a writer whose books are well received.

   A complex sentence contains one independent clause and one or more subordinate clauses (beginning with a word like *which, when, as*).

   Write your own example of a complex sentence.

4. Here are two compound-complex sentences:
   As day turned into night, the stars glistened and the moon beamed.
   I believe voting is an effective way to change government, but my brother disagrees, as you can tell.

   Write your own example of a compound-complex sentence.

Name _____

Date _____

Part D.

Directions: Complete the following steps as you edit your draft.

1. Read your draft aloud. If you find any of the following, circle them on your draft and give each a letter. Write the letters below.

   a. misspellings

   b. errors in subject-verb agreement

   c. errors in pronoun-antecedent agreement

2. Take five consecutive sentences from your composition and copy them in the chart. Identify them according to the four types of structure.

Sentences	Type
a.	
b.	
c.	
d.	
e.	

3. Have you used more than one type of structure?

4. Rewrite one of the sentences here, or combine two to achieve greater sentence variety.

5. Make corrections or changes in your draft, and then check off each point below.

   ____ Is all spelling now error-free?

   ____ Do all verbs agree with their subjects?

   ____ Do all pronouns agree with their antecedents?

   ____ Is there a variety of sentence types, creating a smooth rhythm to the piece?

Name _____

Date _____

Autobiography Evaluation

Directions: Each of the following criteria will be given a score. Use this rubric as a guide while completing your assignment.

Criteria	Points
1. The autobiography is directed at and suited to target audience.	_____ /8
2. The autobiography expresses and fulfills purpose.	_____ /8
3. The topic is appropriate.	_____ /8
4. The autobiography explains how family/event/values are personally significant.	_____ /8
5. The autobiography develops a character/event/future projection with details.	_____ /8
6. The spelling is correct.	_____ /5
7. There is sentence variety.	_____ /5
8. There are no fragments or run-ons.	_____ /5
9. There is subject-verb agreement.	_____ /5
Total Points	_____ /60

Comments:

Lesson 6
Group Publishing Project

Objective

- To select and carry out a plan for publishing the autobiographies

Notes to the Teacher

The completed autobiographies offer students an outstanding opportunity to publish their work to an audience wider than just their small groups. If you feel your students' compositions are not yet ready for publication, you may prefer to postpone publishing projects. Part B of **Handout 8** provides materials to help small groups select a creative publication mode. Monitor groups' discussions and offer sample answers as needed. Allow sufficient time for students to prepare and share final products.

Procedure

1. Put the word *publishing* on the board or on an overhead and have students brainstorm the many ways people "publish" or share their ideas today (*books, magazine articles, letters to the editor, bulletin boards, flyers, booklets, posters, Web pages, audiotapes, videotapes, multimedia presentations, etc.*).

2. Have students complete part A of **Handout 8**.

   Sample Responses:

   1. *Golden Moments at Camp Santa Maria*
   2. *past*
   3. *serious, optimistic*
   4. *gold, green, blue*
   5. *large maple and oak trees*
   6. *horses*
   7. *saddle, bridle, barn*

3. Have small groups share responses to part A.

4. Model how a student might fill in part B after discussing all four stories with the other members of his or her small group.

   Sample Responses:

   1. *childhood memories*
   2. *some serious, others humorous*
   3. *"Childhood Memories of the Class of '99"; one major image for each story*
   4. *large poster with manuscripts and appropriate magazine pictures*
   5. *from earliest to most recent memory*
   6. *poster board, magazines, scissors, glue, magic markers*
   7. *finding appropriate pictures, putting poster together, presenting project to class, displaying poster in media center*
   8. *obtaining materials, typing autobiographies into the computer*

5. Have small groups independently discuss and complete part B.

6. Have small groups complete their projects and share them with the class.

7. Display projects in the classroom or in another appropriate area.

Name _____

Date _____

Planning Our Group Project

Part A.

Directions: Let your ideas flow and allow yourself to be creative as you respond to the following questions about your autobiography.

1. What is your title?

2. What time does your story emphasize?   past   present   future

3. Which of these words describe your story's tone or mood?

    serious   pessimistic   humorous   optimistic

4. What color(s) do you associate with your story?

5. Suggest a plant, flower, or tree image that relates in some way to the story.

6. Suggest an interesting animal image that somehow connects with your story.

7. List any other visual images or symbols that you associate with your autobiography.

Part B.

Directions: In publishing your group's autobiographies, you will make a number of important decisions. Write down ideas about the following.

1. Do your titles have any interesting similarities or differences?

2. Are the stories similar or diverse in time, focus, and mood?

3. What creative group titles and illustrations do your individual images suggest?

4. There are a variety of ways to publish your stories, e.g., booklet, poster, bulletin board, or Web page. Choose one.

5. Arrange the stories in a suitable order and briefly explain your choices.

Author	Title
a.	
b.	
c.	
d.	

6. What materials do you need to complete the project?

7. What steps will your publication process include?

8. Assign specific responsibilities to each group member.

Part 2
Third-Person Narration

In Part 2, students move from first-person to third-person narration as they analyze and write an anecdote. The anecdote is a short narrative designed to crystallize a specific impression. Some anecdotes take the form of jokes that provide comic relief in serious essays or speeches. Others add to the bite in satire, while still others exemplify a person or relationship.

As in the autobiographical lessons in Part 1, students go through the six-activity writing process. Drafting takes place between Lessons 7 and 8. The activities lead to a brief composition, so extended writing time is not necessary. Composing the anecdote enhances writing skills in at least two ways: students practice writing concise, colorful descriptions, and expand the tools necessary for developing extensive compositions later in this unit.

Lesson 7
Introducing Anecdotes

Objectives
- To read and analyze a variety of anecdotes

- To write anecdotes

Notes to the Teacher

Most students are familiar with anecdotes, although they may not know the term. An anecdote is a short, interesting story usually employed to make a point more vivid than a mere statement of facts. An anecdote may be humorous or serious, but it is always a short, concise narration with a definite purpose. Preachers may use anecdotes to emphasize the main point of their sermons. Politicians may use them to add a folksy tone to their speeches. Historians may use anecdotes to characterize some of the great people in history. Nearly everyone who has ever been asked to speak in public begins by catching the audience's attention with a well-chosen anecdote. Students will read and analyze anecdotes, then write their own, providing plenty of opportunity for you to observe and assess their understanding of the subject.

Procedure

1. Write the word *anecdote* on the board and have students tell what they already know about the anecdote form. What are anecdotes? Who tells them today? in what situations? See how much of the information from Notes to the Teacher can be elicited from students and share the rest.

2. Read two or three of your favorite anecdotes aloud to students, as models. Possible sources include *Anecdotes of Destiny* by Isak Dinesen, 1993; *Jazz Anecdotes* by Bill Crow, 1991; *Dave Barry's Greatest Hits* by Dave Barry, 1997; *At Wit's End* by Erma Bombeck, 1988; *Lake Wobegon Days* by Garrison Keillor, 1995; *Presidential Anecdotes* by Paul F. Boller, Jr., 1957; or celebrity anecdotes from the *Overcoming Adversity* Series.

3. Ask students where anecdote writers find their information. Winston Churchill, who often used anecdotes, urged reading history at every chance and recording colorful, amusing anecdotes for later use. Newsstands are full of sources for contemporary history, e.g., *Time, Newsweek, People,* and the daily paper.

4. Distribute **Handout 9**. Ask for volunteers to read each anecdote aloud. After each anecdote is read, discuss the questions that follow. After all the anecdotes have been read and discussed, ask the class what elements the samples have in common. Have them cite examples in each anecdote.

Suggested Responses:

action, people, climax or point of emphasis (purpose), audience

5. Direct students to form groups of four to brainstorm topics for an original anecdote. If necessary, offer the following suggestions.

   a. pleasant or unpleasant surprises at home or in school

   b. shocking incident in the news

   c. family incident

   d. a memorable time spent with a person or pet

   e. any personal experience that demonstrates moral values

6. Tell students that anecdotes may focus on national figures or ordinary people. Give each group a copy of a recent news periodical. Direct them to find striking incidents for use in anecdotes. Have each group share one with the class.

7. Ask students to write a draft of a third-person anecdote (approximately two paragraphs) for the next lesson. Suggest that they use a prewriting organizer to gather their thoughts before writing. A sample organizer and a sample scoring guide for students to have on hand as they write are provided on the Teacher Resource Page.

Original Anecdote

Prewriting Organizer

1. When and where did the incident occur?

2. Who was involved?

3. What problem or situation did they encounter?

4. How did they react? What was the result?

5. What is the point of the anecdote? What does it show?

6. At whom is your anecdote directed? Who would appreciate hearing it?

Scoring Guide

Criteria	Points
1. The anecdote is short and interesting.	____/10
2. The opening explains the background situation.	____/5
3. The sequence of events—who did what—is easy to follow.	____/5
4. The last line sums things up or offers a final thought.	____/5
5. The point of the anecdote is clear.	____/10
Total Points	____/35

Comments:

Anecdote Sampler

Directions: Read each of the six anecdotes below and be prepared to discuss the questions. As you read, ask yourself what these anecdotes have in common.

1. Tale with a sting in its tail

> They called Eleanor Roosevelt "God's gift to newspaper women" because she made it easier for women to get news of the White House, and because she made jobs for them by making much news which only women could get. No previous First Lady held press conferences or gave news directly. Nevertheless, there was painful truth as well as humorous fiction in the Women's National Press Club skit in which a frazzled inmate of the "Eleanor Roosevelt Home for Exhausted Newspaper Women" clasped her hands, and petitioned Heaven: "Dear God, let me pray the prayer they say Franklin [Roosevelt] prays. Just for one day, God, please make her tired! Dear God, just for one day!"[1]

a. How did Eleanor Roosevelt help newspaper women?

b. How did she make their lives tougher?

c. Why would women journalists—and President Roosevelt—want Eleanor to be tired?

d. What was the point of the skit—and this anecdote? Where was the "sting in its tail"?

[1]Edmund Fuller, ed., *2500 Anecdotes for All Occasions* (New York: Crown Publishers, Inc., 1980), 216.

2. Breakfast Brainstorm

Creative people can find inspiration from the most mundane things. Architect Eero Saarinen, for instance, was commissioned in 1956 to design a building for TWA at what is now New York's Kennedy Airport. His first model did not suit him, but he kept working at it. Then one morning at breakfast, he found himself staring at the curved shell of a grapefruit. He turned it over, began carving arches in it, and carried the finished product off to work, adding it to the other models involved in the final design.

When the terminal was completed, it was described by an architectural magazine as "a totality of fluid form curving and circling within itself," suggesting "the flight of a great bird." The grapefruit wasn't mentioned.[2]

a. What was the "breakfast brainstorm" that Saarinen had?

b. What is funny about the last line?

c. How does the story about the architect demonstrate the truth found in the first line?

[2]Carol Orsay Madigan and Ann Elwood, *Brainstorming and Thunderbolts* (New York: MacMillan, 1984) quoted in *Reader's Digest*, May 1968, 161.

3. Advice from Ben Franklin

> When I was a journeyman printer, one of my companions, an apprentice Hatter, having served out his time, was about to open shop for himself. His first concern was to have a handsome signboard, with a proper inscription. He composed it in these words: "John Thompson, Hatter, makes and sells hats for ready money," with a figure of a hat subjoined. But he thought he would submit it to his friends for their amendments. The first he shewed it to thought the word "hatter" tautologous, because followed by the words "makes hats" which shew he was a hatter. It was struck out. The next observed that the word "makes" might as well be omitted, because his customers would not care who made the hats. If good and to their mind, they would buy, by whomsoever made. He struck it out. A third said he thought the words "for ready money" were useless as it was not the custom of the place to sell on credit. Everyone who purchased expected to pay. They were parted with and the inscription now stood "John Thompson sells hats." "Sells hats?" says his next friend. "Why nobody will expect you to give them away. What then is the use of that word?" It was stricken out and "hats" followed it, the rather, as there was one painted on the board. So his inscription was reduced ultimately to "John Thompson" with the figure of a hat subjoined.[3]

a. What general truth or advice is Franklin illustrating here?

b. Is Franklin saying that the sign was better in its shortened form—or that Thompson should not have asked his friends' advice?

c. What sorts of connecting words does Franklin use to help the listener follow the sequence of events?

[3]Ken Macrorie, *Writing to be Read* (New York: Hayden Book Company, Inc., 1986), 25–26.

4. Opportunity/Challenge

The challenge that awaits reminds me of the ancient coat of arms of the royal family of Spain. Before Columbus set sail to cross the Atlantic, it was believed that the world ended out there somewhere past Gibraltar. To the Spanish, one of their real glories was that they were the last outpost of the world, and that their country fronted right on the great beyond. Therefore the royal coat of arms showed the Pillars of Hercules, the great columns guarding the Strait of Gibraltar, and the royal motto said plainly Ne Plus Ultra, meaning roughly, "There is no more beyond here."

But then, when Columbus returned, he had actually discovered a whole new world out there. The ancient motto was now meaningless. In this crisis someone at Court made a noble and thrifty suggestion, which was immediately bought by Queen Isabella. It was simply that the first word, Ne, be deleted. Now the motto on the coat of arms read—and has read ever since—just two words: Plus Ultra—"There is plenty more beyond."[4]

a. What challenge arose and how did the thrifty person at court resolve it?

b. Do you think this anecdote is true? If not, why would someone make up such a story?

c. What sort of challenge do you think reminds the speaker of the coat of arms? How?

[4]James C. Humes, *Speaker's Treasury of Anecdotes about the Famous* (New York: Harper and Row Publishers, 1978), 145.

5. Selfless Scout

      Cub Scout Billy Joe Thomas, of Seattle, is one determined salesman. Working daily six-hour shifts (12 hours on weekends) outside supermarkets and at bus stops—even in pouring rain—he sold 801 tickets to a regional scout show (to the runner-up's 250) and won the grand prize: a trip for four to Disneyland. But Billy Joe had seen a TV program about dying children. Those kids aren't going to have any fun, he thought. Wouldn't it be great to send them to Disneyland? So he gave his prize to two terminally ill youngsters who were chosen by doctors at Children's Hospital and Medical Center in Seattle.

      When word of his selflessness became known, Billy Joe was flooded with awards and letters of praise. Says one scout leader: "Billy Joe thinks that sharing is what scouts do all the time."[5]

a. What does Billy Joe's action show about him?

b. What values does the story emphasize?

c. How does the final line of the anecdote underline the point of the whole story?

[5]"Heroes for Today," *People Weekly*, quoted in *Reader's Digest*, July 1978, 89–90.

6. Believe it . . . or not?

> There is no doubt that certain events recorded at séances are genuine. Who does not recall the famous incident at Sybil Seretsky's when her goldfish sang "I Got Rhythm"—a favorite tune of her recently deceased nephew? But contacting the dead is at best difficult, since most deceased are reluctant to speak up, and those that do seem to hem and haw before getting to the point. The author has actually seen a table rise, and Dr. Joshua Fleagle, of Harvard, attended a séance in which a table not only rose but excused itself and went upstairs to sleep.[6]

a. Anecdotal evidence is often used by social scientists and others to illustrate a point. What is the author's stated reason for sharing the incident at Sybil Seretsky's with his readers? Is that his real reason?

b. Who is Woody Allen's audience? Is he aiming this piece at people who believe in séances?

[6]Woody Allen, "Examing Psychic Phenomena," in *Without Feathers* (New York: Warner Books, 1976), 16.

Lesson 8
One-on-One Conferencing:
A Classroom Laboratory

Objectives

• To give feedback on peers' anecdote drafts

• To receive feedback from a variety of sources

• To increase awareness of the value of conferencing as part of the composition process

Notes to the Teacher

This lesson emphasizes the student's need for one-on-one feedback as part of the writing process. In contrast to the teacher-directed conferencing in Lessons 3 and 4, this approach stresses the reader-reactor's unique, original response to the writing.

Various ways of forming student dyads yield different results. Matching partners of similar ability often provides a rewarding feedback experience for both participants, while pairing a weak student with a stronger one can result in valuable peer tutoring. Allowing friends to choose to work with one another provides a natural collaborative atmosphere, while random pairing can help to provide more objective feedback.

Adult responses contribute alternative perspectives on the student's writing. The lab approach to this lesson frees you to provide expert feedback to individual students and to model effective conferencing behaviors. Feedback from outside the classroom reminds students that writing is not solely a school activity and casts a "real-world" light on the composition.

In preparation for this lesson, students should have completed first drafts of their anecdotes.

Procedure

1. Tell students that most of this day's class time will be spent conferencing one-on-one about their anecdotes. Remind students that the purpose of the activity is to provide supportive feedback to the writer.

2. Have students review **Handout 10**. Arrange students in pairs and direct them to spend ten minutes each in dialogue about each partner's composition, with each reader recording input on the Responder 1 section of the handout. (Note: If the class includes an odd number of students, pair yourself with one student. You will also want to monitor students' conversations to assess their exchanges and intervene in cases of extensive digression, negative emphasis, or focus on editing concerns such as punctuation.)

3. After twenty minutes, stop the conversations. Direct students to seek feedback, either oral or written, from two other people in the classroom, and to record responses in the Responder 2 and Responder 3 sections of the handout. (Note: You may want to tell students not to be distracted by previous responders' feedback.)

4. Encourage students to seek written or oral feedback from you: participate in the conferencing activities by joining partners' interactions.

5. As an assessment of students' ability to process feedback and value conferencing, have students reflect on the process of conferencing and discuss what they have learned about its value. How was it helpful to them? What sort of comments were most helpful? Was it useful to have more than one responder?

6. Ask students to select someone in their families or neighborhoods to be a responder, and to record input under Responder 4 on the handout.

Responses to My Anecdote

Directions: Read your anecdote to your reader. Then allow him or her to read it silently before you ask for an oral response to the four questions below. As the reader shares his or her reactions to your writing, write down the comments.

Responder 1

Name_____

1. What do you like about the way the anecdote is written?

2. Is there anything about the story that is not quite clear to you?

3. What other reactions do you have as you read the anecdote?

4. What suggestions do you have for improving the anecdote?

Responder 2

Name_____

1. What do you like about the way the anecdote is written?

2. Is there anything about the story that is not quite clear to you?

3. What other reactions do you have as you read the anecdote?

4. What suggestions do you have for improving the anecdote?

Responder 3

Name _____

1. What do you like about the way the anecdote is written?

2. Is there anything about the story that is not quite clear to you?

3. What other reactions do you have as you read the anecdote?

4. What suggestions do you have for improving the anecdote?

Responder 4

Name _____

1. What do you like about the way the anecdote is written?

2. Is there anything about the story that is not quite clear to you?

3. What other reactions do you have as you read the anecdote?

4. What suggestions do you have for improving the anecdote?

Lesson 9
Revising and Editing

Objectives

- To revise anecdotes in response to conferencing

- To review how to use commas and semicolons

- To learn and apply ways of achieving sentence variety

Notes to the Teacher

To make conferencing worthwhile, students should evaluate the suggestions offered by others and incorporate some of them. Conferencing is a dialogue, not a monologue, involving reading and listening. Responding to suggestions is an essential step of the writing process, and **Handout 11** guides students through the process of doing so.

This lesson offers questions for essay revision. **Handout 12** also reviews rules for comma and semicolon use, and makes suggestions for sentence variety through inversion. Students need to learn that their words are important, but not indelible. Many of the best writers revise constantly as they consider those criticisms and suggestions that they feel will improve their writing. To help students appreciate that even top writers usually work hard on refining their work, you might share with students what some well-known writers have to say about their own experience with the revision process. For example, in *Speaking for Ourselves* and *Speaking for Ourselves, Too*, edited by Donald R. Gallo, NCTE, several authors of young adult books talk about the importance of rewriting.

Highly recommended for teachers who may wish to explore a range of revision activities, including several that involve listening to comments from others, is Sue Meredith Willis's *Deep Revision: A Guide for Teachers, Students and Other Writers*, Teachers' and Writers' Collaborative, 1993.

Procedure

1. Ask students, "Now that you have done your conferencing and collected suggestions about how to improve your anecdotes, what is the next step?" (*Evaluating the suggestions and implementing some of them comes next. While it is easier to make sentence-level changes, emphasize that some of the changes should be larger, organizational ones that make the piece more unified and coherent.*)

2. Have students complete **Handout 11.**

3. Distribute **Handout 12**. Explain that punctuation and sentence variety are designed to make a writer's ideas more understandable and interesting to others. Before students complete part A, point out that the comma rules discussed are not all-inclusive. Rather than addressing all the other rules, you will discuss them as the need arises. Also, tell students that comma rules are sometimes broken. The most important rules to follow are those that make the writer's meaning clear. For example, a comma splice incorrectly joins two complete ideas with a comma instead of showing the reader where one idea ends and the next begins. Thus, the comma splice muddies the writer's meaning, and is an especially important type of comma error to avoid.)

4. Have students read and complete part A of **Handout 12.**

   Suggested Responses:

   1. *chickens, he*
   2. *cigarettes, magazines, and*
   3. *help," my sister said, "then*
   4. *volunteering, and*
   5. *brother, who . . . friendly, will*

5. Have students complete part B of the handout. Explain to students the similarity between a period and a semicolon, and the slight difference in emphasis between the two. A semicolon signals a pause that is a little stronger than the comma and weaker than the period.

6. Have students complete part C of the handout. Explain that as the model sentences about the summer sun in Alaska show, the same idea can be expressed many different ways. You might draw an analogy between sentence variety and the many different interpretations singers can give the same song or the many different ways artists might render a portrait of the same person. Elicit other analogies from students.

7. Have students use part D as they edit their anecdotes. Emphasize that students should focus first on revising for clarity and coherence, then get down to the "nitty gritty" of sentence and word-level editing (punctuation and mechanics).

8. Direct students to complete final drafts of their anecdotes. **Handout 13** can be used to guide and assess these final drafts.

Name _____

Date _____

Planning My Revision

Directions: You now have suggestions from other people about how to improve your written anecdote. When revising your paper, you should use some of those suggestions to improve it. Remember that careful revision is the mark of a good writer.

Based on your responders' comments—as well as anything you realized as you listened to the comments—answer the following questions.

1. What are the good qualities of my anecdote?

2. What is the one suggestion for improvement that I found most helpful?

3. Is there any suggestion I do not want to use? If so, why not?

4. What parts of the story need to be clarified, more fully described, or reordered?

5. Are there any parts that should be removed from the story because they are unnecessary?

6. Where could I add connecting words to make the links between ideas more clear?

7. Exactly what improvements do I want to make when revising my composition?
   a. beginning

   b. middle

   c. end

Editing Cues

Part A.

Directions: Commas help the reader know where to pause for additional emphasis. The best way to understand commas is to read your paper aloud. The places where you naturally pause—but not stop—are often places for commas. Complete the following as directed.

1. Review the five rules for commas, and add commas where they belong in the five sentences that follow.

   Rule 1 Put a comma before conjunctions such as *and, but, or, nor, for, yet,* and *so* when joining independent clauses.

   I usually eat cereal in the morning, but sometimes I have eggs.

   It hadn't rained in three days, so Derek turned on the sprinkler.

   Rule 2 Put commas between all terms of a series, including the last two.

   My favorite months are June, July, and August.

   Agriculture, architecture, and politics were some of Jefferson's interests.

   Rule 3 Follow parenthetical openers and opening dependent clauses with commas.

   A fine student, Erin is also a skilled athlete.

   Although we often reminisce about the past, we have to live in the present.

   Rule 4 Set off appositives and parenthetical expressions with a comma.

   Mr. Stetson, the mayor of our town, has won re-election three straight times.

   The ice-cream truck, which plays a jingle, attracts many children.

   Rule 5 Set off a direct quote from the rest of the sentence with commas. (Note: Commas, as well as periods, are always placed inside the closing quotation marks.)

   The movers asked, "Where do you want this chair to go?"

   "I am certain," he boasted, "that I will get that job."

   1. When Dave went out to feed the chickens he noticed that the new pony was gone.

   2. The convicted criminal asked for cigarettes magazines and a deck of cards.

   3. "If you aren't willing to help" my sister said "then please wait in the other room."

   4. The old man spent his days volunteering and he spent his nights on the computer.

   5. My big brother who is energetic and friendly will be happy to drive us to the pool.

2. Review your anecdote and correct any comma errors.

Part B.

Directions: Semicolons are used in much the same ways as periods—to separate complete thoughts. A semicolon indicates that the thoughts are closely related. Complete the following as directed.

1. Review the examples that follow.

   Sometimes the second idea is the result of the first.
   A foot of snow fell during the afternoon; rush hour traffic was snarled for hours.

   Sometimes the second idea is an example or elaboration of the first.
   The red-haired girl stood on the corner; she was waiting for her ride.

   Sometimes the second idea contrasts with the first.
   My teacher has a good sense of humor; nevertheless, she can be tough.

2. Examine your anecdote, find one place you could connect ideas with a semicolon, and write the new sentence with a semicolon.

Part C.

Directions: The elements of a simple sentence can be arranged to emphasize different points. Complete the following as directed.

1. Review these variations of the same sentence.

   The summer sun never sets in northern Alaska. (subject-verb-preposition)

   In northern Alaska, the summer sun never sets. (preposition-subject-verb)

   Never sets the summer sun in northern Alaska. (verb-subject-preposition)

2. Take one of the simple sentences in your anecdote, rearrange its elements, and rewrite it.

3. Review these variations of a complex sentence.

   Because the players worked hard in practice, the football team won many games.
   (subordinate clause-main clause)

   The football team won many games because the players worked hard in practice.
   (main clause-subordinate clause)

   The football team, because the players worked hard in practice, won many games.
   (subject of main clause-subordinate clause-verb of main clause)

4. Take one of the complex sentences in your anecdote, rearrange its elements, and rewrite it.

Part D.

Directions: As you edit your draft, fill in the checklist below.

____ 1. Have you read the final draft out loud?

____ 2. Is your purpose clear?

____ 3. Do all details in the anecdote help make the main point?

____ 4. Are the ideas presented in a logical order?

____ 5. Are all words and names spelled correctly?

____ 6. Have all errors in agreement been corrected?

____ 7. Are commas and semicolons used correctly?

____ 8. Is all other punctuation correct?

____ 9. Are sentences varied in length and structure?

____ 10. Is the final copy legible and neat?

Writing 2: Becoming a Writer
Lesson 9
Handout 13

Name _____

Date _____

Anecdote Evaluation

Directions: Each of the following criteria will be given a score. Use this rubric as a guide while completing your assignment.

Criteria	Points
1. The anecdote contains vivid action.	_____ /8
2. The anecdote has one or two characters.	_____ /8
3. There is a chronological order of events.	_____ /8
4. Key details are included.	_____ /8
5. The purpose is fulfilled.	_____ /8
6. The point of the story is sharp and clear.	_____ /8
7. Correct punctuation is used.	_____ /4
8. Correct capitalization is used.	_____ /4
9. The spelling is correct.	_____ /4
10. The sentence structure is correct.	_____ /4
11. There are no uncorrected errors in the publication copy.	_____ /4
12. The cover is attractive and suitable to the subject.	_____ /4
13. The page design is consistent.	_____ /4
14. The column plan is evident.	_____ /4
15. The pictures or drawings are relevant to the story.	_____ /4
Total Points	_____ /84

Comments:

Lesson 10
Reward and Recognition

Objective
- To provide in-house opportunities for group publication of anecdotes

Notes to the Teacher
After you have evaluated the final drafts, have students incorporate any corrections you have made before they submit their papers for display and/or publication. Establish guidelines that will insure a quality display of which writers can be proud. A scoring guide is included that can help assess students' abilities in producing and publishing their booklet.

Procedure
1. Divide students in groups of four to six. Consider grouping them by the type or subject of their anecdotes: family, history, human interest story, neighborhood, animal story.

2. Tell students that they are to design a booklet that will include the contributions of all group members.

3. Distribute **Handout 14**. Have students use part A to collaborate on an interesting cover for their group book. Remind them that the cover should hint at the contents.

4. Have students use part B of the handout to collaborate on page design. If a desktop publishing program is available, encourage students to use it. Many word processing programs, for example, have "newsletter wizards" that offer users step-by-step design choices and enable incorporation of clip art or scanned images.

5. Assign completion of the project as homework. Students may wish to use computers for word processing (which enables experimentation with various fonts and sizes), or they may wish to write out their stories by hand. (Art stores sell stencils, letter stamps, and press-on letters that can also be used for titles.) Students who decide to illustrate their anecdotes might use clip art from graphics programs, glue pictures from magazines, draw simple stick figures, or create more elaborate drawings.

6. As a class, come up with at least four criteria that will be used as a scoring guide to assess the publications.

Sample Criteria
- Cover design is interesting.
- Cover design and title hint at contents.
- Anecdotes by all group members are included.
- Page design is appealing and readable.
- All group members participated in creating the publication.

7. Consider incorporating some of these suggestions for publication of student work.

- Ideas can be found in *35 Ready-to-Go Ways to Publish Students' Research and Writing,* by Michael Gravois (New York: Scholastic, Inc., 1998). Two resources for online publishing are Kathy Schrock's *Guide for Educators* (http://www.discoveryschool.com/schrock guide/) and *How to Publish on the Internet: A Comprehensive Step-by-Step Guide to Creative Expression on the World Wide Web,* by Andrew Fry and David Paul (New York: Warner Books, 1995).

- Contact local newspapers. Some publish student writing on a regular basis.

- Ask your local chamber of commerce about sponsoring a gallery of student writing. Store windows, shopping centers, or malls may serve as display areas.

- Post students' work on your school or school district's Web site. For an example, see Poetry and Fiction from around Nebraska (http://www.esu9.k12.ne.us/~aurora/english/english.html).

Designing Your Booklet

Part A.

Directions: Start to plan your book's size and general cover design.

1. Below are some cover designs. Try your own cover sketches in the spaces provided.

   Examples

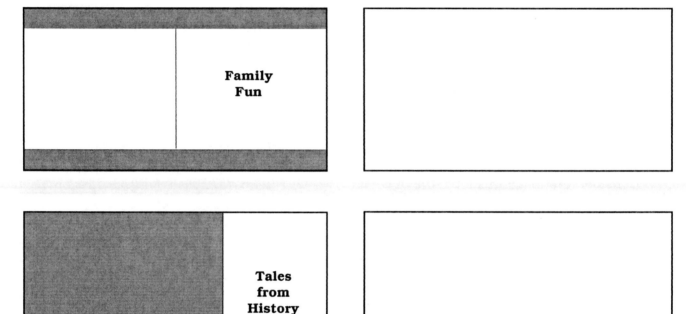

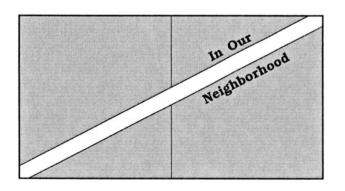
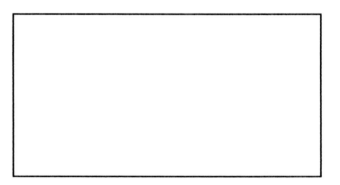

2. Use construction paper, scissors, paste, markers, etc. to make a mock-up of the cover. If you select a magazine picture, be sure it is neatly cut and appropriate for your subject.

Part B.

Directions: Start to plan your page design.

1. Below are some suggestions for page design. Always think of facing pages as one unit of design. All even-numbered pages are on the left, odd-numbered on the right. Only the title page and the last page are single unit designs.

2. Choose the number of columns per page. Set your interior and exterior margins. Arrange the anecdotes in the order in which they will appear. Allow space for any illustrations (and the corresponding captions) that may accompany an anecdote.

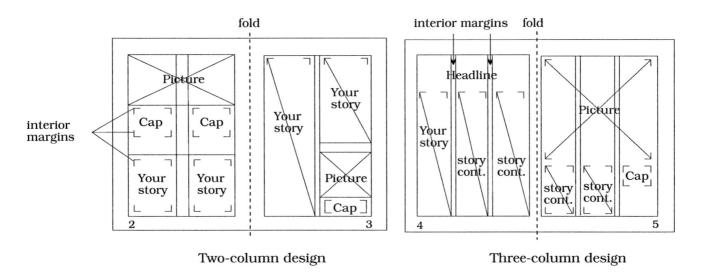

Two-column design   Three-column design

3. Type or print your story in the column width you will use. You can then cut it to fit your space.

Part 3
The Problem/Solution Essay

Students have all experienced problems. They are familiar with what it is like to have a problem and how important it is to seek a workable solution. These five lessons capitalize on that awareness and lead students to write extended essays. Sufficient drafting time will be needed between Lessons 13 and 14.

Problem/solution essays vary in primary focus. Where the problem is generally acknowledged (e.g., the risks associated with nuclear power), writers might well direct most of their efforts toward solutions. When the problem itself necessitates explication (e.g., difficulties in getting insurance companies to make payments), most of the essay might focus on demonstrating that the problem actually exists. Some problem/solution essays propose multiple solutions, some lead to a single recommendation, and still others leave the solution to the reader.

The problem/solution approach is helpful to writers in at least two ways. First, it stimulates careful and creative thinking. Second, it structures itself in two natural divisions.

Lesson 11
Problems, Problems Everywhere

Objectives
- To generate a list of current problems
- To explore creative solutions to problems

Notes to the Teacher
This lesson's prewriting activities prompt students to use their own experiences and the daily newspaper to generate topics for problem/solution essays. You will need to bring copies of recent newspapers so that each student can receive a single page.

Procedure
1. Write the following statements on the board.
   - There is no perfect solution to any problem with human beings mixed up in it.
   - Most people spend more time and energy in going around problems than in trying to solve them.
   - One reason for the world's problems is that we know more ways to get into trouble than to get out of it.
   - Many a problem will solve itself if we forget it and go fishing.
   - Part of the problem today is that we have a surplus of simple answers and a shortage of simple questions.[1]

2. Encourage students to add any quotes or sayings about problem-solving that they may know.

3. Ask students to select one of the quotations and take five minutes to write a reaction.

4. Have volunteers share responses with the class.

5. Ask students to define the word central to all of the quotations: *problem* (*troublesome situation that is not easily solved; any obstacle to our happiness*).

   Ask students to brainstorm a list of problems that affect their lives. If necessary, suggest that students consider problems that they might help solve while fulfilling a service requirement, or problems that people tend to list as ones they most want politicians to address. List brainstormed problems on the board or overhead, and ask one student to keep a clear, complete list for duplication for the class.

6. Point out that problems concern everyone, and that newspapers record many specific examples. Give each student one page of a recent newspaper. Ask the class to peruse the pages for additions to the list of problems that directly or indirectly affect their lives, such as inadequate police protection or air pollution.

7. Have students work in groups of three or four to complete **Handout 15**.

Sample Responses:

Problem—*loss of luggage by airlines*

1. *Arriving at a destination without one's luggage causes, at best, great inconvenience. At worst, it can cause the loss of irreplaceable items.*

2. a. *Allow only handheld luggage.*

   b. *Have separate compartments for passengers to load and unload their own luggage.*

   c. *Have passengers submit complete lists of all packed items and their value; require purchase of insurance, and guarantee immediate permanent or temporary replacement of missing items.*

   d. *Assign personal, specific responsibility for lost luggage tagged with owner's name and flight number.*

   e. *Before takeoff, have a crew member double-check the storage area's contents against a passenger-prepared inventory.*

   f. *Fly only people; insist that all luggage of any type be sent by mail or special carrier.*

   g. *Offer existing loading/unloading crews specific rewards, financial and otherwise, when planes arrive at destinations with all luggage intact; impose penalties when problems occur.*

[1] E. C. McKenzie, *14,000 Quips and Quotes for Writers and Speakers* (New York: Crown Publishers, Inc., 1980), 422–23.

Optional Activity

Introduce students to some graphic organizers they can use as they generate and evaluate solutions.

a. the T-chart

Choice_____

Pros	**Cons**

b. the Decision-making Grid

Problem_____

(Give each solution a rating, 1–5, according to each criterion.)

Possible Solutions	**Criterion 1**	**Criterion 2**	**Criterion 3**
1. _____			
2. _____			
3. _____			
4. _____			
5. _____			

c. the Scale-Balance

Reasons Yes	**Reasons No**
_____	_____
_____	_____
_____	_____

Is this solution a good one?_____

68

Problem and Solutions

Directions: Select a problem that affects your life. Write the problem in the blank and complete the following as directed.

Problem _____

1. Briefly describe the problem. What difficulties or dangers does it involve?

2. Use your imagination as you make up diverse solutions to the problem.

   a. a solution that is too simple

   b. one that is too complicated

   c. a solution that would cause many new problems

d. a very practical, down-to-earth solution

e. one that is extravagant and unrealistic

f. a solution that you think most people would reject

g. one that you seriously recommend

Lesson 12
Professional Models
for Problem Solving

Objective
- To examine different models of problem solving

Notes to the Teacher

Problem solving on national, state, and local levels of life provokes an abundance of satire on TV and in books, magazine articles, and daily newspapers. Writers' witty, humorous, or biting satire on any aspect of the human condition may prod readers to acknowledge the problem, and possibly stimulate a search for a solution.

In this lesson, students are provided with four different approaches to problem solving. Charles Schultz has created a cartoon to express his feelings about world problems and apathy. Art Buchwald and Mike Kilian parody government cover-ups and extravagance. In Buchwald's piece, characters from *Alice in Wonderland* invade a presidential press briefing. Kilian reverses the situation in *A Christmas Carol* by shocking the ghosts of congressmen past as he gives them a guided tour of the present Capitol.

In "Advice for the Hopelessly Absent-Minded," Jack Robinson examines a personal problem shared by many people and offers suggestions on coping with it. Students need to be guided in reading these selections so that they see both the main idea of the writer and how the structure of the essay works to communicate ideas to the reader. Through charts and discussion of these pieces, students' ability to analyze models of problem solving can be assessed.

Procedure
1. Make a transparency of the "Peanuts" cartoon on the Teacher Resource Page and display it using an overhead projector. Ask students to respond to the following questions.

   - What does Sally want to talk about?

   - Do you think she gets the response she expects?

   - What sorts of world problems do you think Sally has in mind?

   - What do you think Charles Schultz may be saying about how most people view world problems?

   - List some examples of being wrapped up in small problems while ignoring bigger ones.

   Allow no more than five to ten minutes for this warm-up exercise.

2. Share the information in the Notes to the Teacher section as you distribute **Handout 16**.

3. Before students read Buchwald's piece explain that the White House press secretary makes periodic announcements to journalists and answers their questions supposedly in order to keep the public apprised of what is going on in the White House. Also make sure that students know what each of these are: *Pennsylvania Avenue, press briefing, transcripts,* and *tapes.* You might note that when this piece was written in 1974, the Watergate scandal, replete with stolen and erased tapes which led to president Richard Nixon's resignation, was a recent event.

4. Have five students read "Alice in Washington" aloud, taking the parts of narrator, Alice, March Hare, press secretary, and Mock Turtle.

5. Ask students these questions to check their understanding of the satire.
   a. What is the first point made by the March Hare?
   (*denial of truth by an official*)

   b. Whom does the chess pawn represent?
   (*press secretary*)

   c. What is the irony of the secretary's response to Alice?
   (*The question he refuses to comment on is the very one he originally posed to her—which she then repeated.*)

71

d. What is the irony of the March Hare's explanation to Alice?
(*The press secretary—chess pawn—doesn't know any answers, but reporters write what he says because it is "official."*)

e. Explain the press secretary's comments on evidence and guilt.
(*See text.*)

f. Why does the press secretary use the Latin words *ergo* and *et cetera*?
(*to fool the audience*)

g. What is the significance of the nonsense poem?
(*Government talks nonsense as cover-up.*)

h. Why is the last sentence a good punch line?
(*Secretary is a pawn, a functionary who has little interest in/knowledge of the situation he is supposed to be explaining.*)

i. How does the dialogue form make the piece more effective?
(*The question/ answer, comment makes the parody more lively.*)

j. Have you ever seen a press conference on television? Have you ever heard press secretaries "deny what they have already told you"? What sort of "riddles" did you hear?

k. Does the reader have to be familiar with Watergate—and with *Alice in Wonderland*—in order to appreciate this piece?

6. Distribute **Handout 17** and have students read part A. There are eight speakers, including the guide and two screamers.

7. Ask students to explain the ghosts' inability to find their way around Washington. Discuss references to women, intelligence of some congressmen, and the significance of the two screamers. Who is the more recent ghost who screams?

8. Have students work in small groups to complete part B. Invite one student from each group report to the class. Ask for any further comments or questions.

9. Distribute **Handout 18**. Have students read it and note differences or similarities between this article and the other two.

10. Distribute **Handout 19** for students to complete. Ask which essays they would choose as a model for their own problem/ solution essay and why?

11. Have students select topics for their problem/solution essays.

"Peanuts"

Fig. 12.1.

Political Satire

Directions: Read the following satirical piece in which Art Buchwald makes fun of a certain aspect of the Washington political scene. Who is the target? What is Buchwald really mocking? Note any reactions or questions, and be prepared for class discussion.

Alice was walking down Pennsylvania Avenue when the March Hare asked her, "How would you like to go to a White House press briefing?"

"What's a White House press briefing?" Alice asked.

"That is where they deny what they have already told you, which is the only reason it could be true," the March Hare said.

"It sounds like fun," Alice said.

The March Hare brought Alice into the press room. A chess pawn was standing at a podium.

"Who is that?" Alice asked.

"That is the press secretary. He talks in riddles. Listen."

"Why are transcripts better than tapes?" the press secretary asked.

"I don't know the answer to that one," Alice said to the March Hare. "Why are transcripts better than tapes?" she shouted to everyone's surprise.

The press secretary looked at her with cold blue eyes. "I refuse to comment on that."

Alice looked confused. "Why did he ask us a riddle if he can't give an answer to it?"

The March Hare said, "They don't tell him the answers; they just give him the riddles."

"What a stupid thing," Alice said. "Why is everyone writing in his notebook?"

"They write down everything he says even though they don't believe him."

"Why don't they believe him?" Alice asked.

"Because he makes things up. He has to or there would be no reason to have a briefing."

The press secretary spoke again. "All the evidence is in and it proves beyond reasonable doubt that the king is innocent of all crimes, ergo, ergo, ergo, et cetera."

"But what about the evidence the king refuses to turn over to the committee?" a dormouse asked.

"That is not evidence," the press secretary replied. "If there was further evidence to prove the king guilty, he would have gladly given it to the committee. The fact that he hasn't turned it over means regretfully there is none. It's as simple as that."

"It doesn't sound very simple to me," Alice said.

"Why can't we hear all the tapes," the Mock Turtle asked, "so we can decide for ourselves who is innocent and who is guilty?"

The press secretary replied, "If you heard the tapes it would only prove the innocent are guilty and the guilty are innocent, and it would serve no purpose but to confuse you. Besides, what you would hear is not what you have read and what you have read is not what you would hear, so it's better not to hear what cannot be read. Isn't that perfectly clear?"

"I feel I'm back at the Mad Hatter's tea party," Alice said.

"Now I will give you some important news today," the press secretary said. "This is on the record. 'Twas brillig, and the slithy toves/Did gyre and gimble in the wabe;/All mimsy were the borogoves,/and the mome raths outgrabe.'"

Everyone wrote it down.

"What did he say?" Alice asked.

"Nothing," the March Hare replied. "He's just stalling until he can go to lunch."[1]

---

[1]Art Buchwald, "Alice in Washington," in *I Am Not a Crook* (New York: G. P. Putnam's Sons, 1974), 77–78.

Satire in Washington

Part A.

Directions: Read the following satirical narration, in which Michael Kilian, like Art Buchwald, lampoons American politics. How have the problems of Congress changed over the years? What is it about the way Congress now operates that Kilian is mocking? Note any reactions or questions, and be prepared for class discussion.

It was a midnight dreary. While I nodded, nearly napping, suddenly there came a tapping, as if someone were gently rapping, rapping at my chamber door.

"Who is it?" I asked, peering outside.

On my lawn, only faintly visible in the misty moonlight, was a group of men wearing very old-fashioned clothes—top hats, tailcoats and the like.

"We are the ghosts of Congresses past," said one of them, who looked remarkably like pictures I had seen of the great Henry Clay. "We want you to take us to the U.S. Capitol."

"Why don't you just go on over by yourselves?" I said. "It's right across the river."

"We can't find it," said another who looked exactly like pictures I had seen of Daniel Webster.

"We can't find anything in Washington we recognize," said another who looked like John C. Calhoun.

Telling my drowsy wife I was taking some ghosts to the Capitol, I set out with the group in tow.

"Things are a little quiet now," I said, as we climbed up the Capitol steps. "All the congressmen and congresswomen are gone after approving the tax increase bill."

"Congresswomen?" asked John C. Calhoun.

"Tax increase?" asked the ghost of James K. Polk, former Speaker of the House. "Can't the government finance itself out of federal land sales?"

"Oh, things come up," said the ghost of one-time congressman Abraham Lincoln. "I had to raise taxes several hundred million dollars to pay for the Civil War."

"This is a trifle more than that," I said. "They increased tax revenues by $98 billion, to reduce the $140 billion deficit and try to keep down the trillion dollar national debt."

Suddenly the night was pierced by a horrible, nerve-rending scream.

"That's just the ghost of Alexander Hamilton," said Henry Clay. "He used to tag along with us on these visits, but I don't think he will any more after hearing what you said."

"What on earth could you possibly think of to spend such an enormous amount of money on?" asked Webster.

"Just look around you," I said. "See those men on the Capitol roof running those American flags up and down? They're paid full time to do that. The flags are sent out to voters."

"This is a function of Congress?" asked James Madison.

"And you see these elevators inside here? I think they had some steam-driven elevators in your time, Mr. Lincoln. Well, these are automatic. But the Congress thoughtfully provides a human operator on them in case a congressman can't figure out how to hit the buttons."

I then took them on to see the House and Senate chambers, which, if larger, were not all that much different than in their day. Daniel Webster even tried out a few lines from his famous "Union Forever" speech from the Webster-Hayne debate.

"Too bad there's no one here to hear me," he said.

"It's almost always like this," I said. "Congressmen and senators like to spend most of their time in their offices."

"Offices?" asked Clay. "Congressmen have offices?"

"Vast suites of offices," I said. "In fact, the Congress has 20 buildings full of offices."

"Extraordinary, sir," said John Quincy Adams. "There must be several thousand members of Congress now."

"No, just 535. But the buildings are necessary. Our senators and congressmen now have 23,000 people working for them. They have to sit somewhere."

"Twenty-three thousand?" said Lincoln. "That's about 43 apiece. What on earth do they do? I had no one working for me when I was in Congress."

"They have all sorts of duties. There was one woman here named Elizabeth Ray who was paid just to—well, she didn't exactly need a place to sit."

"In our days, such women worked in taverns," said Clay. "Not in government."

"These are more generous times," I said. "It now costs more than a billion a year to run the Congress. Let me show you one of the subways. They cost several million to build and let the senators and congressmen ride the two blocks from their offices to the chambers in little railroad cars."

Aghast, the ghosts rode with me on a subway to the newest of the Senate office buildings.

"This is their crowning triumph," I said. "It will house 50 senators. It will have luxurious suites for each, marble walls, a gourmet rooftop restaurant, a squash court, everything. They wanted to put in a $730,000 gymnasium, but they've had to postpone that until after the election. They should have it, though. You really put on the pounds riding subways, sitting in your office, and eating in gourmet restaurants."

"I noticed they've named these buildings after famous members," said Madison. "Who is this one to be named after?"

"One of the most decent, honest, respected and beloved senators of recent times," I said. "He died six years ago. This magnificent edifice is going to be called the Philip Hart Office Building."

Just then I heard another anguished scream.

"Is that Hamilton again?" I asked.

"No," said Webster. "I think it's the ghost of someone a little more recent."[2]

---

[2]Michael Kilian, "The Ghosts of Congresses Past," *The Chicago Tribune*, 1987.

Part B.

Directions: List the ways that the Congress in the article has been wasteful. Then list the ghosts' names and their reactions to these excesses.

Extravagance	Reactor's Name	Reaction

Advice for the Hopelessly Absent-Minded

Directions: Read the following article about forgetfulness. What about it makes you smile? Note reactions or questions, and be prepared for class discussion.

Someone's done it again! Put another article on human memory in front of me. As a "special service," *Newsweek* sent it to its subscribers. I didn't want it. Didn't ask for it.

I've read all the articles and most of the books; I've taken a course on memory. I have reconciled myself to being among the terminally absent-minded. No hope. Drop the subject. Forget it.

But people who have AMS usually also suffer from hyper-curiosity, so I read the article. (AMS stands for Absent-Minded Sufferers. It's time we had a name for it.)

Although the article had no single cohesive theory on why some of us can't remember our kids' names, it did have some interesting facts and theories that backed my single cohesive theory.

Part of my theory is that AMS is biological. It has nothing to do with how much the person cares or pays attention. This is mentioned in the article. A doctor is quoted as saying that maybe the best aid to remembering is to "simply pay more attention." This was my ex-wife's theory, too. And this may be true for most people, but for the AMS afflicted, it's like telling a blind man to turn on more lights.

All scientific evidence (including what's in the article), and all my years of experience with this handicap, all point out the error in this position.

The *Newsweek* article has three proofs of the origin of AMS as biological or neurological. The first is memory's connection with our sense of smell. Some brain structures have triple functions: They handle odor reception, emotions and long-term memory. This explains why odors can evoke strong emotional memories for most—but not all—people. You got it, AMS people's sense of smell not only doesn't do this, it literally stinks. That's why we always have too much cologne on, and why we enjoy the smell of run-over skunks.

The second, and more conclusive, scientific proof in the article is a recent discovery. They can measure a person's ability at "total recall" (which AMS people equate with levitation). Scientists can measure this by recording the length of time a person retains the last-seen image after closing his eyes. One woman could look at one set of dots with one eye, then another set with the other eye, close her eyes and make out the picture these two sets of dots formed when they were put together.

Here's a test to see if you have AMS: Stare at something for a while, a bright light is best, and close your eyes. Almost everyone will keep the image for a few seconds. If what you see is the dark side of your eyelid, welcome to AMS.

The third proof was something new to me. There is a special condition some people have called "prosopagnosia." It means the person absolutely can not recognize faces. My position is that prosopagnosia isn't that rare. There are degrees of this condition. Most AMS people can remember a face—as long as it hasn't put a hat on, changed its color of hair or makeup or changed its surroundings or hasn't been out of sight too long. I have completely misunderstood movies where the heroine had changed her hairdo half-way through it.

Don't get me wrong; people with AMS can have good memories. When meeting a nameless person we know, we can recall whole conversations with them; we know their problems, their triumphs and their characters. But we may just walk by them without recognizing them. Unless a movie is very well done, I can't stand to watch it twice. I can predict the dialogue of all the actors, including the first and second heroines.

There *is* something biological about AMS. It's time our scientists got on this. Something else they could check out: It has some connection with the inability to do crossword puzzles, and something to do with having zero sense of direction.

My second contention is that AMS is hereditary. This can be proved by simply looking at my own family. My mother went to her grave at 73 without having ever straightened out her five boys' first names. My younger son averages four trips from the car to the house and one trip up the driveway before he's pretty sure he's got almost everything he'll need to take with him. My daughter has found her car keys in less than 20 minutes exactly twice in the past 14 months. Taking into account all my brothers, uncles, aunts, and all their families, everyone in my entire family will be looking for something sometime today.

My last, and most disheartening conclusion, is that AMS is terminal. There is no cure. Psychological tricks don't work. The Dale Carnegie course teaches how to visualize the face as describing the name, like Mr. Bannano will have a banana for a nose. This merely proves that Dale can not only remember faces, but faces with bananas on their noses.

Six months after taking the course I ran into one of the people I had been through "remembering faces and names" drills with for three months. After both of us failed at our attempts to dodge each other, we stood right in the middle of the shopping mall and laughed at these two "what's their names."

Here are some home remedies for the symptoms of AMS. You'll be able to receive the full list of these remedies this fall when I begin my television ministry.

1. Don't bother to even buy gloves or hats. For the little bit of body surface they keep warm, they simply are not worth all the time, effort and frustration.

2. Always have paper and pencil. The moment anything is said or occurs that is going to require action on your part, write yourself a note. Never, ever put these notes anywhere but in your pocket until either you've done what they say, or you find you've read them too late to do what they say. Throw them away immediately after they've been done or it's too late to do anything about them.

3. Each evening, or whenever you change clothes, empty your pockets at one chosen spot. Put it all onto one pile. Include your belt, watch, and notes in this pile.

4. Each morning, or every time you dress, put on all your clothes then go to the pile. Fill your pockets, belt loops and wrist. Read all notes, and either do what they say, put them back into your pocket, or swear out loud and throw them away.

5. While at home, pile things you need to take with you (as you find out you need them) between you and the door. Always go out the same door. Look down.

6. Take up smoking. This way, while at work, what you need to take home with you can be piled on top of your cigarettes (you can't leave all these things between you and the door). Always light up before leaving anywhere.

7. Make up unusual habits to make you remember things. Like patting yourself down like a detective every time you stand up to leave somewhere. Like always opening doors with a hand full of keys. Pause at every exit and ask yourself, "Am I forgetting something"?

   While some of these habits may be a little embarrassing at first, they are nowhere near as embarrassing as borrowing flashlights and enlisting the aid of strangers in looking for things.

   And they may take some time to learn, but they will save you hundreds of hours in the end.

   A good example: While working my way through school, I often slept in two shifts. I then sped off either to work or to school. Work was east of the interchange, school was north. Seventy-two percent of the time I went the wrong way. Solution: Put my wallet in my left hand (if north to school) right hand (if east to work), before allowing myself to enter the car. Keep it there until making the right choice. It took two months to learn not to get into the car until I figured out where I was going, then put my wallet in the appropriate hand, but the wrong-way trips were cut to 14%.

8. Practice greetings like: "Hi, how 'ya doing?" or "What you been up to?" or better yet, ask something about your last conversation. Never put yourself in the position of having to introduce people to your family. Teach your children to wander off when you are approached by someone with a big smile. Even if you can drag up the name of your kid, you'll never remember the smiling face's name.

   But, most importantly, remember that AMS is biological, inherited and incurable, not a social or personal failing. Wander around with pride. Never mind the wife. And maybe someday the scientific community (I think it's near Newark) will come to our aid.

   Who knows? Maybe specially marked parking spaces at shopping centers. They don't have to be close to the stores. We don't mind walking a long way to the entrance.

   It's the ordeal of looking casual and purposeful while wandering up and down the rows looking for our damn cars that breaks down our arches, makes our children lose faith in us, our wives leave us, and contributes to our eventual painful, lonely and tragic early deaths.[3]

[3]Jack R. Robinson, "Advice for the Hopelessly Absent-Minded," *The Plain Dealer*, 29 May 1987, B9.

Name _____

Date _____

Comparing and Contrasting

Directions: Complete the following chart based on what you have read.

Author	Form of Humor	People Targeted	Problem	Solution
1. Charles Schultz	visual humor, sarcasm			
2. Art Buchwald	parody of Lewis Carroll biting satire/ dialogue			
3. Michael Kilian	parody of Charles Dickens biting satire/ dialogue			
4. Jack Robinson	tongue-in-cheek mockery narrative/list			

Lesson 13
Exploring a Topic

Objective
- To explore problem/solution topics

Notes to the Teacher
The problem/solution essay lends itself to "lateral thinking," a term coined by Dr. Edward de Bono to describe a cognitive approach seeking many solutions to a single problem and new alternatives to old patterns. This lesson instructs students to generate solutions to their essay topic problems—anything from the practical to the extravagant. Then students examine the pros and cons of each solution and determine the more feasible ones. These new skills can be assessed using student responses to **Handout 20**.

Procedure
1. Demonstrate and explain the idea of "lateral thinking" by placing an object (a lacrosse stick, for example) in front of the class and asking, "How many ways can you think of to use this?" As students generate answers, point out that they have found many solutions to a single problem—and that they have come up with new alternatives to old uses. They have used lateral thinking.

2. Point out, too, that some of the solutions are more practical than others. (You could use a lacrosse stick to paddle a canoe, but the holes in the net make it less effective than an oar.) While the first stage in solving a problem is often brainstorming possible solutions—without stopping to evaluate whether they are good or bad—the next stage needs to be evaluating the relative utility of each one.

3. Explain that this lesson is designed to help students explore the problem/solution topics they chose at the end of Lesson 12. They have already gone through the process of generating problems and selecting one. Now they need to examine possible solutions, and consider the strengths and weaknesses of those solutions.

4. To demonstrate some techniques for evaluating various solutions, you might take the "drippy chocolate" problem from the "Peanuts" cartoon (Lesson 12, Teacher Resource Page), generate three solutions as a class, list the pros and cons of each solution, then rank the solutions from one to three.

5. Distribute **Handout 20** and use the board or overhead to model how to complete it. Encourage students to use their imagination and sense of humor.

6. Have students complete **Handout 21** and write their own satires.

7. Have students complete first drafts of problem/solution essays. You might suggest this optional framework:

   Paragraph 1: Introduce the problem. What is the problem—and why is this a problem?

   Paragraph 2: Examine weakest solution. What are the pros and cons?

   Paragraph 3: Examine stronger solution. What are the pros and cons?

   Paragraph 4: Examine the best solution. Why is this the best?

   Paragraph 5: Summarize. What are you proposing? Leave readers with a thought to remember.

Problem/Solutions

Directions: Complete the following to help you organize your thoughts about the topic you have chosen for your problem/solution essay.

1. What is the problem you will be discussing in your essay?

2. Who is your essay's target audience?

3. List three solutions to the problem.

    a.

    b.

    c.

4. a. Name three good points and three bad points of your first solution.

Good	Bad

    b. Name three good and three bad points of your second solution.

Good	Bad

c. Name three good and three bad points of your third solution.

Good	Bad

5. Rank your solutions from 1 (most workable) to 3 (least workable).

   Solution 1:

   Solution 2:

   Solution 3:

6. Briefly explain why you think the highest-ranked solution will work.

Your Satire

Directions: Everyone enjoys a good laugh—and satire is often a good vehicle for conveying problems that need attention. Answer the following questions to help you begin in writing a satirical problem/solution paper.

1. Think of satire you enjoy, including that found in newspapers (columns and cartoons), on television (comedy and talk shows), on the Internet (newspaper parodies), on the radio (monologues, songs) and in humor magazines. List some of your favorites.

2. Think of some of the topics upon which your favorite contemporary satirists have chosen to focus their wit. List some of these.

3. What are some of the topics that authors, such as Mark Twain and Jonathan Swift have chosen to lampoon? How might one of their classics be contemporized?

4. What events in the daily and school news do you feel strongly about? List a few.

5. What problem in contemporary life would you choose as the target of your satire?

6. What will be the primary purpose of your satire? Is it to make people aware of the problem by making the situation seem ridiculous? Is it to point out why the direction now being taken will not lead to a good solution?

7. As you have seen from the models in Lesson 12, satire can be biting or fairly gentle. It can be direct (the speaker addresses the reader) or indirect (storytelling). What style will you use?

8. Good satire is not overwhelmingly angry. It is funny and it is accurate (even if there is exaggeration). It usually targets a group or a practice, rarely an individual. How will you "set the stage" in your piece to make your point humorously?

9. What facts will you include? What will you exaggerate?

10. Like Art Buchwald and Mike Kilian, you might choose to parody a well-known story or poem or write a spin-off. If you were to make your point by incorporating certain parodic elements into an episode of a television show (e.g., *The Simpsons*), how might you do that?

11. How might you publish this piece? Would you submit it to your school newspaper? post it on a personal Web site? enter it in a writing contest?

Lesson 14
Conferencing Opportunities

Objectives
- To develop conferencing skills through large-group feedback experiences
- To increase awareness of what might go into a good problem/solution composition

Notes to the Teacher
Writing specialists often emphasize the value of having writing teachers attempt the assignments they give their students. The benefits include original models for classroom review and hands-on awareness of the demands of specific assignments. The best material for procedure 1 of this lesson is your first draft of an original problem/solution essay, either duplicated or on an overhead transparency. Besides giving students a glimpse of your writing style, the conferencing session also provides an opportunity for you to model constructive responses to praise, questions, criticism, and suggestions and assess student response to them. If necessary, **Handout 22** may be substituted for your original essay.

In preparation for this lesson, students will need working drafts of their problem/solution essays. You will need duplicated copies or overhead transparencies of two or three volunteers' compositions.

Procedure
1. Ask students to participate in a large-group conferencing session. Distribute **Handout 22** or your first draft. Have students read it and write comments and questions in the margins.

2. Direct the conference by asking:

   a. Could you give me some general reactions first? What do you like about this?

   b. Is the nature of the problem clear? Is the problem real?

   c. What about my solutions? Are they creative? diverse?

   d. Is my tone appropriate to these proposed solutions?

   e. Do you have any questions about my ideas?

   f. How do you respond to my writing style?

   g. Do you have any other comments, suggestions, or criticisms?

   Promote the use of concrete comments such as

   - You chose a good problem and your essay is easy to follow.

   - You do not seem to include a serious solution to this real problem.

   - You could develop your paper more completely by examining other alternatives. I like your use of specific details.

3. Direct large-group conferencing of two or three volunteers' compositions. Encourage a focus on the content and clarity of the work.

4. Have partners or small groups meet to conference about the rest of the students' problem/solution drafts.

5. Provide individual teacher-student conferencing for students who request it or for students who would benefit from special assistance.

6. Have students revise drafts of problem/solution essays. Provide the following list of transitions, and suggest that students consider inserting one or more to improve clarity by helping readers follow the connections between ideas.

   - one
   - another
   - a second
   - a third
   - finally
   - the effect

   - as a result
   - consequently
   - therefore
   - more important
   - most of all
   - last but not least

A Problem/Solution First Draft

Directions: In preparation for a large-group conferencing session, read the draft below about a problem at the writer's high school. As you read, note your reactions (comments and questions) in the margins. Evaluate how well the writer has presented the problem and possible solutions. Think about elements you can praise, as well as suggestions you might make for improving the piece.

Hawkins High School is a reasonably nice facility with many advantages, swimming pool, little theatre, and double gym, among others. The building does, however, have one major liability. It is not air-conditioned and the windows face east and west, with the result that hot days in September and May make students and teachers feel as if they are working in a kiln. It is not unusual for people to faint during a class. Hardier specimens may become very irritable, while even the most dedicated may lose their interest in learning anything except techniques for staying cool in the tropics.

One sultry September, the Student Council decided to address this problem. After a week of meetings, conducting student polls, and recording the actual temperature in various school rooms (105° in a third floor chemistry room!) the officers reached a conclusion and sent a recommendation to the principal. Their solution: furnish air-conditioning throughout the building. Attractive as that notion may seem, the astronomical cost of cooling our rambling three-story building makes any reasonable person reject this solution as overly extravagant. After all, the mercury does not soar every day in September and May.

Another solution was proposed by a local school board member. Confronted by an angry son, who left a sweltering school building to visit his father's refrigerated office, Mr. X suggested that the students conduct a fund-raising campaign to finance the air-conditioning of key areas in the building. The suggestion seemed like a good one until discussion revealed diverse opinions on what constitutes a "key area." Freshmen seldom appreciate air conditioning in a faculty room; a cooled library may not be a top priority for a physical education teacher; what English teacher is really distressed by the heat in the industrial arts room?

As I sit here in American history on September 24, the sun is blazing through the window, and the hall thermometer reads 95°. The humidity must be about 99.9%. The desk surface is tacky, and perspiration is dripping down my neck. Surely the conditions can be described as severe, and I suggest that we handle this situation the same way we deal with other extreme weather. Heavy snowfall leads to "snow days," and the extreme cold necessitates "cold days." In many places, torrential rainfalls lead to weather emergency school closings because of flood danger. Here at Hawkins, we need a system of "hot days." When the mercury climbs over 90°, let's cancel classes and proceed to cooler, more pleasant haunts: Edgewater Beach, a shopping mall, or the air-conditioned living room at home.

Lesson 15
Editing

Objectives

- To use precise, lively verbs

- To place colons correctly

- To edit drafts

Notes to the Teacher

Specific nouns and strong verbs lay the foundation for all powerful writing. In particular, verbs—the engines that drive sentences—supply the movement and momentum in writing. Writers get mired in linking verbs and passive constructions, never realizing the energy available in other verbs. Of course, students do not need to eliminate all forms of the verb *to be* (or of those other overused linking verbs *become, seem, smell, look, grow, feel, sound, get, taste, appear*). However, they should learn to be selective in their use and to find stronger alternatives.

This lesson also discusses the colon, an infrequently used but effective stylistic device. Certain situations require a colon: others are a stylistic preference. Use your judgment about emphasizing its use. **Handout 23** can help assess the need for such emphases.

Procedure

1. Distribute **Handout 23** and review the use of effective verbs together before students complete part A independently.

2. Go over the answers to part A and have volunteers share some of the changes they made in their own verb use while editing their problem/solution papers.

3. Have students examine your teacher-written draft (or **Handout 22**) and suggest instances where verbs could be replaced.

4. Review the use of the colon before students complete part B independently.

5. Go over the answers to part B and have volunteers share sentences with colons from their problem/solution papers. Have students discuss which version—with or without colons—would most effectively convey the student writer's ideas.

6. Direct students to incorporate what they have learned about effective verbs and correct colon usage as the complete the final draft of their problem/solution essays. **Handout 24,** an evaluation rubric, can be used to guide and assess these final drafts.

Optional Activity

Offer mini-lessons on subject-verb agreement (Lesson 5) as well as on common irregular verb forms, avoiding improper tense shifts, and/or sentence clues to appropriate verb tense. Students with a demonstrated need could then focus on one or two of those problems while editing their problem/solution papers.

Editing for Energy

Part A.

Directions: Read the information about effective verbs and complete the following as directed.

We all like movement—leaves falling, athletes racing, the ocean crashing. We also like action and movement in our writing. One of the first tools to consider when writing an interesting essay is the verb. These "action words" power the entire sentence, making it fast or slow, loud or quiet.

1. Compare these two versions of the same sentence. Why is the second version better than the first?

   a. The oak tree *moved* and *made noises* as the night wind *made a loud sound.*

   b. The oak tree *swayed* and *rustled* as the night wind *roared.*

2. Your writing slows down or even grinds to a halt if you use too many linking verbs (*become, seem, smell, look, grow, feel, sound, get, taste, appear* and *forms of to be*). Rewrite the following sentence, replacing *is* with a more interesting, precise verb.

   The teenager *is* in the chair.

3. Your writing will also become bogged down if you overuse the passive voice. Which of the following sentences has more zest?

   a. The seven-story World Bank building was scaled by a man yesterday.

   b. A man scaled the seven-story World Bank building yesterday.

4. Replace each italicized verb with one that is more lively and precise.

   a. The cat *went* across the busy street and *sat* under a bush.

   b. "Say it ain't so, Joe," a tearful boy reportedly *said* to his hero.

   c. The flood waters *came* through the area, forcing residents to *run* for their lives.

5. Each sentence below is in the passive voice. Switch the verb around and rewrite the sentence so that it is in the active voice.

   a. The metallic cargo pants and diamond-strapped heels were tried on by Cathy.

   b. The tray of pizza and soda was dropped by the unfortunate waiter.

   c. The underwater camera was tossed into the water by Lucy.

6. Reread your problem/solution draft and replace any dull, lifeless verbs that you find with better ones. Write one of the sentences you changed below. Cross out the verb(s) you changed and write the new verb above it.

Part B.

Directions: Read the information about colon usage and complete the following as directed.

The colon often means "as follows" or "as a result." Used effectively, it can add variety and energize halting sentences. Colons are used

- To introduce a long or formal quote

    The Declaration of Independence begins: "When in the course of human events . . . "

- To introduce a list of items

    You should see the stuff in Donnie's pockets: a yo-yo, a candy wrapper, a baseball card, a shell, and two sticks of gum.

- After the salutation of a business letter

    Dear Sir or Madam:

- To separate hours from minutes

    10:33 A.M.

- To introduce a short phrase or clause that explains and illustrates a preceding statement.

    Only one-third of the people voted: apathy is on the rise.

A colon introduces one idea that helps explain the other, while a semicolon connects two separate but closely related ideas. The difference is not always clear, but reading the sentence aloud will often help you use your best judgment.

Place colons wherever appropriate in the sentences below.

a. It was clear what the other team was trying to do hurt people, not play hockey.

b. Several factors account for the line's resurgence continuity, scheming, attitude, luck, and a new quarterback.

c. Their key player overslept the team lost.

d. Just look at the numbers the company has sold 1.6 billion of the open-and-eat boxes since they were introduced eleven years ago.

e. A strange affliction has overwhelmed my mother since I got my driver's permit the total loss of her sense of humor.

Reread your problem/solution draft and find a passage where you might have used a colon, but did not. (Feel free to add ideas.) Write old and new sentences below.

Name _____

Date _____

Problem/Solution Evaluation

Directions: Each of the following criteria will be given a score. Use this rubric as a guide while completing your assignment.

Criteria	Points	
1. Each paragraph has a main idea.	_____	/8
2. The style and content is suited to the target audience.	_____	/8
3. The problem is clearly stated.	_____	/8
4. The writer demonstrates knowledge of the subject.	_____	/8
5. Workable solutions are presented.	_____	/8
6. Creative solutions are presented.	_____	/8
7. Any satirical or exaggerated solutions make a point.	_____	/8
8. The mechanics are correct.	_____	/4
9. There is sentence variety.	_____	/4
10. Action verbs are used.	_____	/4
11. Transitions are smooth.	_____	/4
Total Points	_____	/72

Comments:

Part 4
Exposition

Part 3 introduced students to expository writing by focusing on problem-solving. In this section, they have the opportunity to expand to other modes of development. Multiple patterns and subjects lend themselves to this very flexible form.

These five lessons incorporate the six-stage writing process towards an extended composition. Ample drafting time will be needed between Lessons 18 and 19. The revision activity in this section builds on conferencing experiences. Leave time for revision between Lessons 19 and 20.

During this section, students examine the devices of comparison/contrast and paradox, both of which can contribute effectively to expository development. You will want to encourage, but not require, the incorporation of one or both of the techniques in the essay product.

Lesson 16
A Sample Essay

Objective
- To examine a sample essay for underlying structure

Notes to the Teacher

As Daniel O'Neil writes in *Book about Books,* "An essay is like a battered old hat in the closet of literature." Like an old hat, it is a comfortable form that can be worn at any angle, punched into different shapes according to the wearer's purpose. From Plato and Aristotle, to Montaigne to Erma Bombeck, humans have been writing essays. Whether the essay is a serious, factual investigation in literature, history, science, or math, or a strong expression of an opinion on any topic under the sun, it reflects its author.

Even an old hat has a form or structure. Likewise, the essay that is clear, cogent, and concise often has a simple but distinctive pattern: the Aristotelian beginning, middle, and end. Students learn to identify these patterns through a sample essay.

Procedure

1. Ask students what magazines they read. List them on the board, leaving space for topics of individual articles.

2. Have volunteers cite recent favorite articles they have read. List them under magazine titles.

3. Ask the class how many like to read essays. (*Very few hands will go up.*) Then say, "But you just told me about your favorites. Except for fiction, poetry, and drama, magazine articles *are* essays, examples of expository writing. Newspaper editorials are essays of opinion. Feature articles are also essays which present an author's special view of a person or situation."

4. Share background information from Notes to the Teacher.

5. Review the following vocabulary words: *communications satellites, revolution, transmission, obsolete, information storage and retrieval, linguistic barriers, national pride,* and *technology.*

Allow about fifteen minutes for discussion of these questions:

- Over the past millennium, what inventions have had the most impact on our ability to communicate with each other?

- What are communications satellites? What do you already know about how they affect our lives?

- How do you think new developments in the "information superhighway" will make life different fifty years from now? What will be obsolete? Will we speak the same languages as today?

- Do you ever read online books/newspapers, or communicate online? Do you think these will ever replace "hard copies" and libraries and phones? Would that be a good thing?

- Do you agree or disagree with the following statement? Why?

   Most of the traveling that now takes place—including going to the workplace—could be avoided with better communications.

6. Distribute **Handout 25** and tell students to compare their own thoughts and predictions with those made by Arthur C. Clarke, a noted science fiction writer, as they read his essay. Encourage students to put a check mark or make any comments beside any idea or choice that appeals to them. As they read, they should be aware not only of what Clarke is saying, but how he is organizing his essay. Have students jot responses to the handout questions.

7. Conduct a class discussion of the essay's content and structure. Project a transparency of Clarke's essay and indicate logical transitions. Review students' responses to the handout questions.

Suggested Responses:

1. *Clarke points out that communication of unlimited ideas has been a distinguishing human characteristic, the "agent of civilization" leading up to the most powerful means of communication today: the satellite.*

2. *paragraphs 3, 4, 5*

3. *telephone, travel*

4. *Though answers will vary, students should offer pros and cons to support their views.*

5. *Instant information, instant replay; unlimited access to the whole world of information; in the Central Library storage system, scholars and students would be able to call up any information from any age by pressing buttons.*

6. *Students should summarize the advantages Clarke gives in paragraphs 12–13 and speculate on some disadvantages.*

8. *Time zones—the round globe makes them necessary.*

9. *Students should summarize paragraphs 20–22, analyze pros and cons, and offer an opinion.*

10. *If we make our machines so much smarter than ourselves, what use will they be to us?*

8. Culminate the discussion by asking students to respond to the following items.

- Trace the flow of Clarke's thought from his introduction through the body of the essay.

- Summarize what Clarke says about history, and explain what function the introduction serves. Then have them point out what he says about the consequences of future communications satellites—for the good or ill of humanity. List pros and cons, explain why some items might belong in both categories.

- What is the final thought with which Clarke leaves the reader? Does he think that the instruments of communication which have served us will become our masters? Do you?

- When was this piece written? To what extent have some of Clarke's predictions (e-mail, working at home, newspapers and books on the Internet) come true? To what extent is the piece dated?

9. Tell students to generate three possible topics for their own expository essays. They might consider using Clarke's piece as a model and writing about another scientific development that is already changing our lifestyle.

Thoughts of the Future

Directions: Read Arthur C. Clarke's essay, in which he speculates about what the future will be like thanks to communications satellites. As you read, think about both the content and the structure of the essay. Mark the copy by underlining, circling, or noting questions and comments whenever you are struck by a phrase or idea. Respond to the questions that follow the essay, and be prepared for class discussion.

Beyond 1984: The Social Consequences of Communications Satellites

1   In the ability to communicate an unlimited range of ideas lies the chief distinction between man and animal; almost everything that is specifically human arises from this power. Society was unthinkable before the invention of speech, civilization impossible before the invention of writing. Half a millennium ago the mechanization of writing by means of the printing press flooded the world with the ideas and knowledge that triggered the Renaissance; little more than a century ago electrical communication began that conquest of distance which has now brought the poles to within a fifteenth of a second of each other. Radio and television have given us a mastery over time and space so miraculous that it seems virtually complete.

2   Yet it is far from being so; another revolution, perhaps as far-reaching in its effects as printing and electronics, is now upon us. Its agent is the communications satellite.

3   It is not necessary to go into technicalities to appreciate why such satellites can transform our communications. Until today, the reliable range of radio has been limited to a few score of miles, for the simple reason that radio waves, like light, travel in straight lines and so cannot bend round the curve of the Earth. The only thing that makes long distance radio possible at all is the existence of the ionosphere, that reflecting layer in the upper atmosphere which bounces back the so-called short waves so that they reach the ground again at great distances from the transmitter. In the process they usually acquire considerable distortion and interference; though they may be adequate for speech, they are almost useless for music, as anyone who has listened to a concert on the short-wave bands knows.

4   For the still shorter waves, which alone can carry television and other sophisticated types of telecommunication service, the situation is even worse. These are not reflected back from the ionosphere at all, but slice straight through it and out into space. They can be used, therefore, only for what is called line-of-sight transmissions; you cannot (except under freak conditions) pick up a television station from much farther away than you could see it in perfectly clear air. This is why television transmitters, and the microwave relays now used to carry hundreds of simultaneous telephone circuits across the country, are all sited on towers or mountains to obtain maximum range.

5   Satellites allow the communications engineer to place his equipment, in effect, on the top of a tower hundreds or even thousands of miles high. A single satellite-borne transmitter could broadcast to almost half the Earth, instead of to an area fifty miles in radius; three of these, spaced equally round the equator, could provide any type of communication service between any two points on the globe.

6   This may have as great an effect on business and social life as the invention of the telephone itself. Just how great that was, we of today have forgotten; perhaps we can remind ourselves by imagining that the

telephone was suddenly abolished and we had to conduct all business face-to-face or else by correspondence carried by stagecoach and sailing ship. To our grandchildren we will still seem in that primitive level of development, and our present patterns of daily commuting a fantastic nightmare. For ask yourself how much traveling you would really have to do if you had an office in your own home equipped with a few simple information-handling machines and wide-screen, full-color television through which you could be in face-to-face contact with anyone on Earth. A good nine-tenths of the traveling that now takes place could be avoided with better communications.

7   There can be no doubt that satellites will have an especially great effect on the transmission of written and printed information. One idea that has been discussed at some length is the Orbital Post Office, which may make most air mail obsolete in a decade or so. A single satellite, using modern facsimile equipment, could easily handle the whole of today's transatlantic correspondence. Eventually, letters should never take more than a few minutes to be delivered to any point on the Earth, and one can even visualize the time when all correspondence is sent by direct person-to-person facsimile circuits. When that time comes, the post office will cease to handle letters, except where the originals are required, and will concern itself only with parcels.

8   Another development that will have the most far-reaching consequences is the Orbital Newspaper; this is inevitable once the idea gets around that what most people need is information, not wood pulp. Half a century from now, newspapers as we know them may not exist, except as trains of electronic impulses. When you wish to read *The New York Times*, you will dial the appropriate number on your channel selector, just as today you call a party on the telephone. The front page would then appear on your high-definition screen, at least as sharp and clear as on a microfilm reader; it would remain there until you pressed a button, when it would be replaced by page two, and so on.

9   Of course, the entire format would be completely redesigned for the new medium; perhaps there would be separate channels for editorials, book reviews, business, news, classified advertising, etc. If you needed a permanent record (and just how often do you save your daily paper?), that could easily be arranged by an attachment like a Polaroid camera or one of the high speed copying devices now found in all modern offices.

10   Not only the local paper but all the papers of all countries could be viewed in this way, merely by dialing the right number—and back issues, too, since this would require nothing more than appropriate extra coding.

11   This leads us directly into the enormous and exciting field of information storage and retrieval, which is one of the basic problems of our culture. It is now possible to store any written material or any illustration in electronic form—as, for example, is done every day on video tape. One can thus envisage a Central Library or Memory Bank, which would be a permanent part of the world communications network. Readers and scholars could call for any document, from the Declaration of Independence to the current bestseller, and see it flashed on their screens.

12 The most glamorous possibility opened up by communications satellites is the one which I originally stressed in 1945—global radio and television. For the first time one nation will be able to speak directly to the people of another, and to project images into their homes, with or without the cooperation of the other government concerned. A Londoner, for example, will be able to tune into NBC or CBS or Radio Moscow as easily and clearly as to the BBC. Most of us will see the day when every home will be fitted with radio and TV equipment that can tune directly to transmitters orbiting thousands of miles above the Earth, and the last barriers to free communications will be down.

13 Quite apart from its direct visual impact, the effect of TV will be incomparably greater than that of radio because it is so much less dependent on language. Men can enjoy pictures even when they cannot understand the words that go with them. Moreover, the pictures may encourage them to understand those words. If it is used properly, global television could be the greatest force yet discovered for breaking down the linguistic barriers that prevent communication between men.

14 Nobody knows how many languages there are in the world; estimates run to as high as six thousand. But a mere seven are spoken by half the human race, and it is interesting to list the percentages. First by a substantial margin comes Mandarin, the language of 15 percent of mankind. Then comes English, ten per cent. After that there is a large gap, and grouped together round the five percent level we find in this order: Hindustani, Spanish, Russian, German, and Japanese. But these are mother tongues, and far more people understand English than normally speak it. On the basis of world comprehension, English undoubtedly leads all other languages.

15 Few subjects touch upon national pride and prejudices as much as does language, yet everyone recognizes the immense value and importance of a tongue which all educated men can understand. I think that, within a lifetime, communications satellites may give us just that. Unless some synthetic language comes to the fore—which seems improbable—the choice appears to be between Mandarin, English, and for obvious reasons, Russian, even though it is only fifth on the list and understood by less than five percent of mankind. Perhaps it will be a photo finish, and our grandchildren will be bi- or trilingual. I will venture no predictions, but I would stress again that it is impossible to underestimate the importance of communications satellites in this particular domain.

16 Though there are obvious dangers and possibilities of friction, on the whole I am very optimistic about this breaking down of national communications barriers, holding to the old-fashioned belief that in the long run right will prevail. Communications satellites can bring to every home on earth sadism and pornography, vapid parlor games or inflated egos, all-in wrestling or tub-thumping revivalism. Yet they can also expose lies and spread the truth; no dictatorship can build a wall high enough to stop its citizens' listening to the voices from the stars.

17 These are some of the obvious and predictable effects of communications satellites, but there will be others much more subtle that will have even more profound effects upon the structure of our society.

18 The fact that the world is round and it is thus noon in Washington when it is midnight in Mandalay inconvenienced nobody in the leisurely days before the airplane and the radio. It is different now; most of us have had to take overseas phone calls in the middle of the night or have had our eating and sleeping schedules disrupted by jet transport from one time zone to another. What is inconvenient today will be quite intolerable in ten or twenty years as our communications networks extend to cover the globe. Can you imagine the situation if in your own town a third of your friends and acquaintances were asleep whenever you wanted to contact them? Yet this is a close parallel to what will happen in a world of cheap and instantaneous communications, unless we change the patterns of our lives.

19 We cannot abolish time zones, unless we beat the Earth into a flat disc like an LP record. But I suggest, in all seriousness, that the advent of global telephony and television will lead to a major attack on the problem of sleep. It has been obvious for a long time that we can't afford to spend twenty years of our lives in unconsciousness, and many people have already stopped doing so. You can now buy a little box that keeps you in such deep slumber, through electronic pulses applied to the temples, that you require only one or two hours of sleep per day.

20 This suggestion may seem to be fantasy; I believe it barely hints at some of the changes that communications satellites will bring about. What we are building now is the nervous system of mankind, which will link together the whole human race, for better or worse, in a unit which no earlier age could have imagined. The communications network, of which the satellites will be nodal points, will enable the consciousness of our grandchildren to flicker like lightning back and forth across the face of this planet. They will be able to go anywhere and meet anyone at any time, without stirring from their homes. All knowledge will be open to them, all the museums and libraries of the world will be extensions of their living rooms. Marvelous machines, with unlimited information-handling capacity, will be able to speak directly into their minds.

21 And there's the rub, for the machines can far outpace the capacities of their builders. Already, we are punch-drunk with the news, information, and entertainment that bombard us from a thousand sources. How can we possibly cope with the far greater flood to come, when the whole world—soon, indeed, the whole solar system—will be clamoring for our attention?

22 The communications network we are building may be such a technological masterpiece, such a miracle of power and speed and complexity, that it will have no place for man's slow and limited brain. In the end there will be a time when only machines can talk to machines, and we must tiptoe away and leave them to it.

1. Consider how Arthur C. Clarke develops his essay in three main parts—beginning, middle and end. What function does the first paragraph serve? How does it prepare us for his main idea, which is in paragraph 2?

2. Clarke uses contrast—presentation of differences—to develop his main idea. In what paragraphs does Clarke contrast the satellite's power with the limitations of radio and TV in the past?

3. Clarke also uses cause and effect to develop his ideas. According to Clarke, what are two other current modes of communication that may be drastically altered in the future, thanks to the development of satellites?

4. The satellite's power will not only change oral communication, but also may transform transmission of the written word. Would you like to see an "Orbital Post Office" (paragraph 7) become a reality? Why or why not? What would happen to personal privacy? national security?

5. Paragraphs 8, 9, and 10 extend and explain the idea in paragraph 7. What advantages are there to having massive information and retrieval systems in an Orbital Newspaper?

6. Clarke gives us several interesting ideas to consider. Like any good essay writer, he offers "food for thought" to the reader who asks, "So what?" Do you think that global television or radio, as Clarke describes it, will improve human relationships? Why or why not?

7. Clarke weighs pros and cons in an effort to persuade us that his predictions and opinions are valid. From "linguistic barriers" the narrative moves to a consideration of multiple languages (paragraphs 13–16). What will happen to the many families of language, according to Clarke? How do you feel about this? Do you think Clarke's balancing of positive and negative factors is realistic?

8. Clarke uses a one-sentence paragraph (paragraph 17) as a visual marker. The paragraph serves as a transition between obvious influences of the communication satellite and its more profound effects on our personal lives. How does geography play a strong role here?

9. Rather than give a dull rehash of his ideas, Clarke ends his essay with interesting speculation about the implications of what he has said. Where does he start this "winding down"? Is the world unity envisioned by the author desirable? List disadvantages as well as advantages.

10. Clarke's conclusion, whether you agree with it or not, is effective it contains a note of finality while encouraging the reader to mull over what he has said. What is Clarke saying about our technology versus our human nature?

Lesson 17
Comparison/Contrast and Paradox

Objectives
* To analyze examples of comparison/contrast and paradox

* To write brief examples of comparison/contrast and paradox

Notes to the Teacher
Comparison and contrast are two sides of the same coin. One or the other usually dominates, depending on the topic. In exposition, comparison/contrast can serve as a helpful tool in developing and clarifying ideas. Similarly, the paradox, an apparent contradiction that is somehow true, can be a powerful tool in writing. Both comparison/contrast and paradox can serve as central organizing principles; they can also be used as specific supportive detail.

This lesson introduces both devices as forms of figurative language; students then examine literal applications and learn to create their own through models offered in **Handouts 26** and **27**.

Procedure
1. Draw a large Venn diagram (two overlapping circles) on the board or overhead and elicit from students what such a diagram is often used for (*comparison/contrast of two things, with shared elements placed in the overlapping region*).

2. Tell students that comparison/contrast can be an effective tool for developing and expressing ideas. You might read a good example from the editorial page of your daily newspaper.

3. With students, list examples of topics they may have developed through comparison/contrast in various subject areas. For example:

   * in a history class—similarities and differences between the League of Nations and the United Nations

   * in a science class—how plants and animals are alike and different

   * in a magazine—differences between two popular musical groups

   * in a discussion—the relative merits of a Caribbean cruise and a ski trip to Switzerland

   * in literature—similarities and differences between Shakespearean and Petrarchan sonnets

4. Have students complete **Handout 26**. You might actually read passages by Homer, Sandburg, and Dickinson—either the ones used as examples, or others containing figurative comparisons. You also might want to offer a prose example, such as this passage from Mark Twain's *Martin Chuzzlewit*.

   > Mrs. Todgers was a lady, rather a bony and hard-featured lady, with a row of curls in front of her head, shaped like little barrels of beer.

5. Have students complete **Handout 27,** part A. Discuss their answers.

   Suggested Responses:

   1. *attitudes toward life in the Middle Ages and the Renaissance*

   2. *differences*

   3. *The Middle Ages emphasized life after death; the Renaissance emphasized life in this world.*

   4.

Middle Ages	Renaissance
• *cathedral towers*	• *signed art pieces*
• *unsigned art pieces*	• *portraits of artists*
• *representation of Christ child*	• *representation of Christ child*

   5. *difference, but, not only, but also, in the first period, in the second period*

   6. *The author could deal with all Middle Ages material first, then all Renaissance material second.*

6. Before having students complete part B of the handout, introduce them to paradox, which is a seemingly contradictory statement that is actually true. (*"My life closed twice before its close."*)

7. Have students complete part B of **Handout 27**.

   Suggested Responses:

   1. *examples about obeying laws, voting, gullibility, art and music*

   2. *law: we claim law and order values, but see no problem in individually breaking laws, such as speed limits*

   3. *America's paradoxical nature; discrepancy between ideals and actions; America seems charming but immature*

8. Present students with a high-interest example of an essay topic that might be developed by comparison/contrast (e.g., "Compare and contrast what two different states are doing to reduce the high car accident rates among teenage drivers") and of a topic that might be developed by use of paradox (e.g., "Teenagers are rebels who try hard to conform"). Encourage students, as they further think through exposition topics, to brainstorm other ways of using comparison/contrast and paradox.

Optional Activity

Have students bring in examples of comparison/contrast: in newspaper headlines, bumper stickers, company slogans, etc., for display in the classroom.

Comparison/Contrast and Paradox: Figurative Language

Part A.

Directions: Read the information about developing and organizing ideas through comparison/ contrast. Then answer the questions.

Poets often use comparisons as ways of compressing expression for increased impact. Consider these:

- In the *Iliad,* Homer compares a troop of soldiers riding into battle to a herd of cattle rushing over a dry plain. How do you think the soldiers and cattle are alike?

- In the poem, "Chicago," Carl Sandburg compares the city to a "tall, bold slugger." How do you think Chicago might be like a baseball player?

- In the poem, "I like to see it lap the Miles," Emily Dickinson compares a train to a horse that races and neighs its way across mountains and valleys. How do you suppose the train is like a racing horse?

Figurative comparisons are also effective in prose.

1. How might you develop each of these comparisons in a prose passage? Write your ideas in the Venn diagram.

   a. a woman and a spider

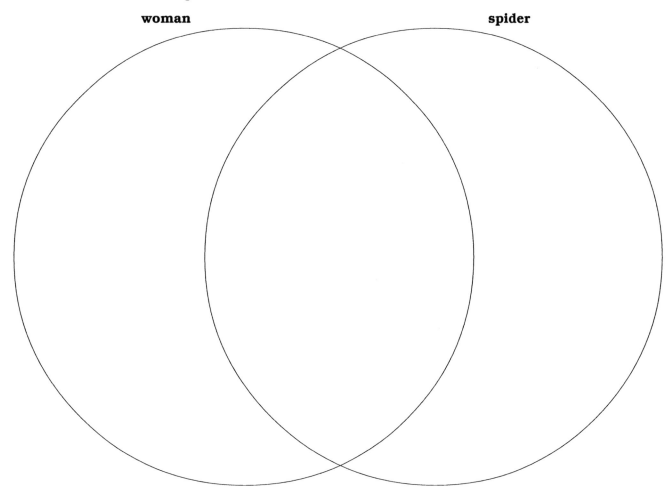

b. a committee meeting and a circus

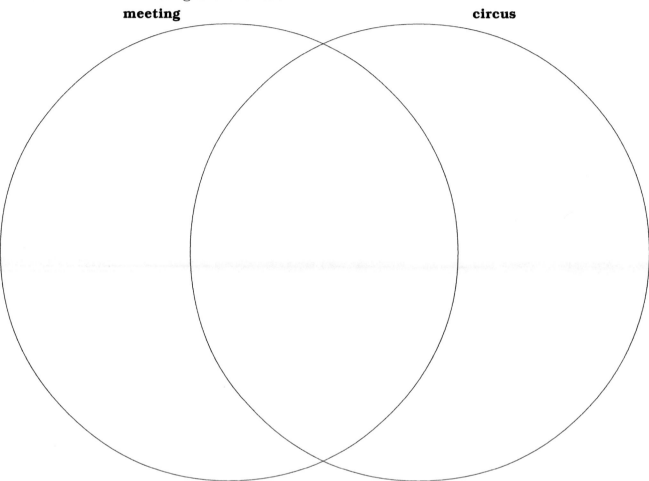

2. List people, places, things, and events that might be compared/contrasted (e.g., athletes, amusement parks, types of sneakers, sporting events).

Part B.

Directions: Paradox is an apparent contradiction that is somehow true. Like comparison/contrast, paradox can be an effective figurative device for developing and organizing ideas. Put each example into your own words and respond to the questions.

1. What is the contradiction and the truth in these two sentences?

   a. Latin literature includes this paradox: When he is silent, he screams.

      Paraphrase

   b. Thomas Hardy, British poet and novelist, notes that a soldier at war kills a person he would ordinarily enjoy joining for a drink.

      Paraphrase

2. What do you imagine in your mind's eye as you read each of the following examples of paradox?

   a. She was happily depressed for a week.

      Paraphrase

   b. He hurts the ones he loves.

      Paraphrase

   c. Only those who don't search for happiness find it.

      Paraphrase

3. What are three paradoxes about people, places, things, and events you know?

Comparison/Contrast and Paradox: Literal Language

Part A.

Directions: Like poets, expository writers use comparison and contrast to develop and organize ideas. Read the passage about the Renaissance, and answer the questions that follow.

> Life! The filmstrip, "The Renaissance—the Age and Its Art," shows the startling difference between attitudes toward life in two very different periods—the Middle Ages and the Renaissance. In the Thirteenth Century the vaulted towers of the great cathedrals pointed to the spirit world, life after death. Renaissance art showed interest in man's existence in this world—the life of his senses and of nature. Medieval artists did not even leave their names. But, in the Renaissance, men were seeking fame and fortune in this world. They left not only their names, but also their portraits. In the first period, the Christ child is pictured as a miniature adult, and the background scenes of nature are imaginary and unreal. In the second period, Christ is a real baby, and the backgrounds of nature are portrayed with almost scientific accuracy. Yes, the Renaissance emphasized life: individual, human life in this world as lived by real men in a real, sensual world.
>
> —John Hess

1. What topics are being compared and contrasted?

2. Does the paragraph emphasize similarities or differences?

3. What is the main point in the comparison/contrast?

4. What supportive evidence is included? List details in the chart below.

Middle Ages	Renaissance

5. What words are used to signal that ideas are being compared/contrasted?

6. The writer organized his ideas this way: Middle Ages/Renaissance; Middle Ages/Renaissance; Middle Ages/Renaissance. What other organizational approach could he have used?

Part B.

Directions: As you read the following passage from "America and Americans," look for the paradox. Then answer the questions.

> The paradoxes are everywhere: We shout that we are a nation of laws, not men—and then proceed to break every law we can if we can get away with it. We proudly insist that we base our political positions on the issues—and we will vote against a man because of his religion, his name, or the shape of his nose. . . .
>
> We fancy ourselves as hard-headed realists, but we will buy anything we see advertised, particularly on television; and we buy it not with reference to the quality or the value of the product, but directly as a result of the number of times we have heard it mentioned. The most arrant nonsense about a product is never questioned. We are afraid to be awake, afraid to be alone, afraid to be a moment without the noise and confusion we call entertainment. We boast of our dislike of highbrow art and music, and we have more and better-attended symphonies, art galleries, and theaters than any country in the world. We detest abstract art and produce more of it than the rest of the world put together.
>
> —John Steinbeck

1. Explain the apparent contradiction of some of the specific paradoxes Steinbeck mentions?

   a. our attitude toward laws

   b. how we vote

c. how we respond to advertisements

d. our cultural tastes

2. Select one of the four examples above, and explain how the statements/actions can be true and contradictory.

3. What seems to be Steinbeck's main point?

4. Steinbeck observed that Americans' behavior can be paradoxical. Note three paradoxical observations you have made about your fellow Americans (or classmates).

a. _____ , but _____ .

b. _____ , but _____ .

c. _____ , but _____ .

Lesson 18
Topic Generation and Thesis Development

Objectives

- To brainstorm, narrow, choose, and cluster essay topics

- To compose a focused thesis statement based on the chosen topic

Notes to the Teacher

Exposition is the umbrella term for any essay that defines, analyzes, and/or explains. As the most common type of essay in high school and college, its mastery is important for students' academic success.

One of the toughest aspects of writing is getting started. As Byron once said, "Nothing so difficult as a beginning." You might encourage students to examine topics directly germane to their lives: family, academics, friendship, sports, work, ambitions, travel, dating; or topics of a broader, more communal scope: society, education, politics, industry, religion, economics, technology.

In this lesson, **Handout 28** helps students use brainstorming and clustering to produce and organize their initial ideas. If students are familiar with clustering (also called "mapping" and "webbing"), briefly review the process; if not, a fuller explanation will be necessary (See *Writing 1*, Lesson 7; "Brainstorming: Let the Ideas Flow").

Because of the vast range of exposition topics, the writer's next job is to narrow the focus. **Handout 28** also involves students in creating a focused thesis statement (See *Writing 1*, Lesson 20; "Beginning Essay Writing: Thesis Statement").

Students then write the first draft of their essays and conference with three readers about how to revise the drafts. Students with specialized topics may need to have access to people familiar with their topics for conferencing.

Procedure

1. Have students complete part A of **Handout 28**. Here, private brainstorming precedes group work. Encourage students not to give up after seven ideas; brainstorming, like all aspects of the writing process, sometimes requires that extra push.

2. Have students share brainstormed ideas and add to their lists.

3. Before students complete part B of the handout, review what a thesis statement is and how to narrow one down. Be sure students understand that a good thesis statement does for an essay what a good topic sentence does for a single paragraph: it points the way for the entire piece. Every detail in the essay should somehow support that thesis. Furthermore, the thesis should be a statement about the topic—often a statement of how the writer feels about a problem or an issue around which people have different opinions.

4. Have students complete part B of the handout. Discuss with them how important it is not only to generate topic ideas, but to narrow that topic down. Topics should be general enough that students can find plenty of ideas with which to support it—but not so general that they could write a book about it! Have students suggest several possible thesis statements they could write about the topic of lifeguarding—and evaluate which ones are too general or too specific. (*"Lifeguarding is a job that many teenagers get over the summer"* is probably too general and *"Lifeguarding is a job that offers good pay"* is probably too specific.) Finally, have them vote on some thesis statements that are "just right"—not too general, not too specific.

5. Review the essay assignment described in part B. Set a reasonable deadline for students to complete essay writing and conferencing (such as a week to write the draft and three days for the conferencing, one day per reader).

111

Brainstorming and Planning

Part A.

Directions: Read the information below, and then brainstorm some topics for the expository essay you will be writing.

What should I write about? You have asked that question many times and probably have struggled over it. Selecting an essay topic is often the most difficult decision of the writing process. Did you ever try turning the steering wheel of a parked car? Sometimes, when you can't decide on a topic, that's the way you may feel about writing—lots of effort with no result. Once you do decide, however, the writing gets much easier, just as turning a steering wheel does when the car is in motion.

Here are three tips for choosing a topic:

1. Write about something important to you. Writing allows and encourages expression. You and your ideas are the focus of every essay you write. An essay provides a unique opportunity for you to state those ideas and for others to respond to them. If your essay excites you, that enthusiasm will liven up your words. If not, your essay will be a struggle to write and a chore to read.

2. Write about something you know. Knowledge is more interesting than ignorance. Unless you are eager to explore new ideas, choose an essay topic within your area of expertise or strong opinion.

3. If you cannot think of one topic, think of ten. In other words, if you are not going anywhere, go everywhere. This approach is called brainstorming. Write down any topic, even peculiar ones. Do not force and do not fight; let your mind freely move from one idea to another. (Sometimes it helps to do something first that jogs your thinking, such as flipping through a newspaper for topics that interest you, talking to friends, listening to arguments, watching the television news, taking a walk, etc.)

Brainstorm ten or more topics for your expository essay and write them below.

Part B.

Directions: Read about clustering below. Then follow the steps to write your expository essay.

You might know clustering as "mapping" or "webbing." To cluster a word or idea, write it down, circle it, and then draw radiating lines around it. On these lines, write down any word or phrase that comes to mind when you hear that center word. Do not judge these associations as "good" or "bad" at this point. New ideas might generate others, or you might return to the central idea.

Here is an example of clustering the topic "lifeguarding."

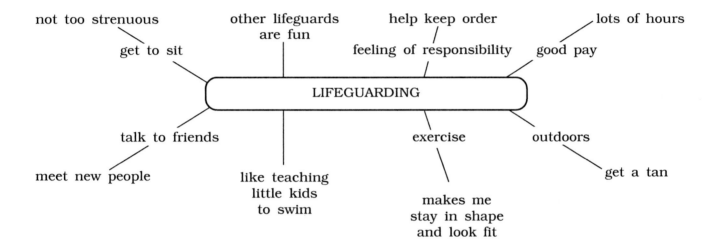

From the cluster, you could write a general (thesis) statement and supporting ideas.

Thesis Statement: Lifeguarding is an excellent summer job.

Supporting Details: 1. Improves responsibility
2. Improves social life
3. Improves physical fitness

Note: Not all cluster ideas need to be used in your final essay.

1. Select a topic, write it in the middle of a piece of paper, draw radiating lines around it, and cluster your ideas.

2. Review your cluster and write a general thesis statement. This should be a statement about your topic—a statement with which some people might disagree.

3. List at least three supporting ideas (examples or reasons).

4. On separate paper, expand each supporting idea into a paragraph. Do this by taking the supporting idea as your topic sentence and writing at least three sentences that explain or defend that idea. These three (or more) paragraphs are the body of your essay.

5. On separate paper, write an introductory paragraph for your essay. Suggest your thesis: Let your reader know what your topic is and where you will be taking it. Give the reader some real information, not just vague generalities. Get the reader interested in listening to what you are about to say.

6. Write a concluding paragraph for your essay. Do not rehash what you have already said. Leave your reader with an interesting thought about all you have said. Wrap up by making it clear why you have bothered to address this topic at all! Sometimes you can neatly tie together the beginning and end of your essay by concluding with an idea or detail that you mentioned in the introduction. Sometimes you might end with an interesting quote.

Part C.

Directions: After you have written your essay (introduction, at least a three-paragraph body, and conclusion), give it to three readers: a classmate, a person familiar with the subject, and a third person of your choice. You may use the five questions below, or others of your own. Keep notes on readers' responses.

1. What do you like about my paper?

2. Is the paper well-organized? Can you point out places where one idea does (or does not) connect clearly with the next?

3. Do I seem to know the subject well? Where should I have included more support?

4. What will you remember the longest about this paper?

5. What are your suggestions for improvement?

Lesson 19
Conferencing

Objectives

- To summarize readers' comments after conferencing

- To respond to other students' essays

Notes to the Teacher

Expository essays teach and strengthen organizational skills. This lesson uses the conference time for evaluating essays on organizational grounds—the clarity of topic and supporting sentences, the unity and coherence of paragraphs, smooth transitions, and a clear conclusion. Meanwhile, other writing skills—such as forceful verbs, sentence variety, and proper mechanics—are assumed to be emphasized. In the previous lesson, students have received comments about their essays, largely about content. This lesson's focus on organization should give students ample feedback for substantial revisions and ample opportunities to assess their ability to give and receive constructive criticisms.

Procedure

1. Have students complete part A of **Handout 29**.

2. Direct students into group conferences. Have students silently read each other's essays and complete part B of the handout.

3. Have groups dialogue about each member's essay, using the readers' reactions as a basis for suggestions.

Name _____

Date _____

A Feedback Summary

Directions: Summarize the comments of all three readers about each area below. Wherever you have listed suggestions for changing your draft, mark those you plan to use (+) and those you do not plan to use (-).

Title of My Paper: _____

Names of My Three Readers: _____

1. Good Points

2. Organization

3. Knowledge of subject

4. Suggestions for improvement

Part B.

Directions: Let members of your group silently read your essay. Have them use this chart to record reactions, observations, or suggestions.

Comment	Reader 1	Reader 2	Reader 3
a. The main idea is clearly stated.			
b. The supporting ideas are clearly expressed.			
c. Each paragraph has a clear purpose.			
d. All paragraphs are relevant.			
e. There are smooth transitions between paragraphs.			
f. The conclusion is clearly stated.			
g. Additional notes			

Lesson 20
Editing

Objective
- To edit for word economy and passive voice

Notes to the Teacher

There is much more to editing than correcting errors in grammar, usage, and mechanics. Another important challenge for young writers is stylistic improvement. One technique for enlivening writing is to practice word economy. One method for reducing wordiness while adding vigor and conviction is to switch from passive to active voice.

Whether to use active or passive voice is an artistic decision and sometimes the passive voice is, indeed, preferable (for instance, when students are writing certain sections of a science lab report). To make that decision, students first must become aware of what verb voice they are already using. **Handout 30** assesses students' awareness of voice and word economy, and contains a final editorial checklist.

Procedure

1. Put two statements on the board or overhead, one active and one passive.
   - The weather channel shows reruns.
     Reruns are shown on the weather channel.
   - I ate the last cookie.
     The last cookie was eaten by me.

2. Explain what *active voice* and *passive voice* mean. Ask students where they have seen the passive voice used (*scientific report, legal paper, history text; situations where someone was being evasive*).

3. Point out that students should use the active voice in most of their writing because it is usually more direct and vigorous than the passive voice. Journalists, for instance, write primarily in the active voice and rarely use phrases such as *there is* or *could be heard*. Offer students several sentences from the daily paper and have them recast the sentences in the passive voice. See if students agree that the active voice is bolder and often more concise. Note: In the classic *Elements of Style*, William Strunk states that using the active voice is one of the elementary principles of composition. For a complete discussion—as well as examples of cases where the passive voice may actually be more convenient—consult *Elements of Style*. It is available online (http://www.bartleby.com/141/index.html).

4. Point out that there are other ways to omit needless words from writing. Put this sentence on the board or overhead and ask students how to make it more concise.

   I was unaware of the fact that I had left my clarinet in the chemistry lab.

   Suggested Response:

   I was unaware that I had left my clarinet in the chemistry lab.

5. Have students complete **Handout 30**, part A. Have volunteers share revised sentences.

   Suggested Responses:

   1. *Late-night snacks create fat and clog arteries.*
   2. *Microwave beeps wake others in the house.*
   3. *You hear nosy people who know about your diet snicker.*
   4. *You grab some crackers and slurp down spoonfuls of ice cream.*

6. Assign part B. Allow sufficient time for students to revise any passive-voice sentences in their drafts.

7. Have students complete part C. Ask volunteers to share their work

   Suggested Responses:

   1. *I am not singing because I have laryngitis.*
   2. *Procrastination is a problem I will tackle later.*
   3. *Losing the homecoming game surprised no one.*
   4. *My brother, an attacker, just scored the winning goal.*

8. Have students use part D of the handout to apply what they have learned about writing concisely to their drafts.

119

9. Direct students into group conferences. Have students silently read each other's essays, using the editing checklist in part E to find any errors in grammar, usage, or mechanics.

10. Direct students to complete final drafts of their essays. **Handout 31,** an evaluation rubric, can be used to guide and assess these final drafts.

Active/Passive Voice and Word Economy

Part A.

Directions: Read about active and passive voice. Then practice changing some statements from the passive voice to the active voice.

Editing becomes easier, and sometimes even more enjoyable, after you have mastered certain rules of grammar. Then you can concentrate on improving your style—expressing your ideas through more dramatic and creative language. As you know, good writing requires effective, precise verbs. Often your writing will be stronger if you replace a verb in the passive voice with one in the active voice.

Passive: The watch was given in appreciation of his many years of service to the company.

Active: The company gave him a watch in appreciation of his many years of service.

The active voice expresses the idea more concisely. To find passive verbs, look for these items:

    a. a helping (auxiliary) verb (usually a form of *to have been*)

    b. a past participle (*carried, thrown, discovered*)

    c. the word *by* (The pier was battered *by* the waves.)

1. Fat is created and arteries are clogged by late-night snacks.

2. Others in the house are awakened by microwave beeps.

3. Snickers are heard from nosy people who know about your diet.

4. Some crackers are grabbed and spoonfuls of ice cream are slurped down by you.

Part B.

Directions: Complete the following steps to revise your essay.

1. Examine your essay and circle any passive verbs you have used. Write the sentence(s) on a separate piece of paper.

2. Change the sentences into the active voice and rewrite the sentence(s).

3. Compare the revised sentence(s) to the original one(s). Choose the one you think is better and briefly explain why.

4. Make the change(s) on your draft.

Part C.

Directions: Read about omitting needless words. Then practice making some sentences less wordy.

Changing from passive to active voice is one way to eliminate extra words. Removing certain unnecessary, redundant phrases is another.

Wordy: He is a person who knows how to change the oil owing to the fact that his father taught him.

Concise: He knows how to change the oil because his father taught him.

1. I am not singing owing to the fact that I have laryngitis.

2. Procrastination is a problem which I will tackle later.

3. The fact that we had not won the Homecoming game surprised no one.

4. My brother, who is an attacker, just scored a goal, which was the winning one.

Part D.

Directions: Complete the following steps to revise your essay.

1. Examine your essay and circle any sentences that contain needless words. Write them on a separate piece of paper.
2. Rewrite each sentence so that it is more concise.
3. Compare the revised sentence(s) to the original one(s). Choose the version you think is better and briefly explain why.
4. Make the change(s) on your draft.

Part E.

Directions: Have a classmate help you edit your essay. Here is a checklist.

____No fragments   ____Correct spelling

____No run-ons   ____Subject-verb agreement

____Correct capitalization ____Pronoun-antecedent agreement

____Correct punctuation

Name _____

Date _____

Expository Essay Evaluation

Directions: Each of the following criteria will be given a score. Use this rubric as a guide while completeing your assignment.

Criteria	**Points**	
1. The style and content are suited to the target audience.	_____	/8
2. The essay expresses and fulfills a purpose.	_____	/8
3. The main idea is clearly stated.	_____	/8
4. Supporting ideas are included.	_____	/8
5. Each paragraph has a clear purpose.	_____	/8
6. All paragraphs are relevant to the main idea.	_____	/8
7. Comparison/contrast and/or paradox are used appropriately.	_____	/8
8. The writer demonstrates knowledge of subject.	_____	/8
9. The conclusion is clearly stated.	_____	/8
10. The mechanics are correct.	_____	/4
11. There is sentence variety.	_____	/4
12. Action verbs are used.	_____	/4
13. Transitions are smooth.	_____	/4
Total Points	_____	/88

Comments:

Part 5
Description

This section provides activities to encourage development of descriptive passages. The result is not an extended composition, but a collection of short writings. All three of the lessons include prewriting strategies; Lesson 23 also suggests a publishing activity. The other four writing activities are placed squarely in the hands of the student writer.

As a mode in its own right, description stresses the sights, sounds, tastes, smells, and tactile sensations associated with the subject. It can also be a powerful supportive tool in other modes of writing.

Effective description depends on sensitive perceptions and precise word choices. It requires constant alertness to purpose, so that the description enhances the writing rather than detracts from its overall effectiveness. Remaining aware of one's audience helps to prevent causing boredom with too much—or too little—descriptive detail.

Lesson 21
Careful Observation and Colorful Description

Objectives

- To explore sense perceptions as a basis for vivid description

- To write descriptions that include both dominant impressions and specific details

Notes to the Teacher

The art of description, based on the art of observation, requires an ability to transcend the trite and hackneyed. Only by taking time to explore sense impressions and to experiment with the vagaries of denotation and connotation can young writers learn to compose verbal re-creations of experience.

For this lesson, you will need enough kinds of fruit (pear, strawberry, kiwi, grapes, avocado), so that each group of students receives a different one. You may want to bring napkins and a knife. You will also need a slide or a large picture of an interesting scene involving people. You can find this in art posters (like "The Boating Party"), photograph books (such as Margaret Bourke-White's, *You Have Seen Their Faces*), sports posters, or an art museum Web site such as The Louvre (http://www.louvre.fr/louvrea.htm).

If students' past writing experience has included a description based on fruit, you may want to replace the fruit with small animals (goldfish, hamsters), sculptures (wire, clay), candies (gummy worms, mints), or other items. **Handout 32** can serve as an assessment of students' ability to explore sense perceptions and record them in descriptive paragraphs.

Procedure

1. Tell students that this lesson will focus on the art of description. Read them one or two short, vivid examples of well-written description containing sensory details. (This could be anything from a restaurant review in your newspaper to a page from a novel. Many Young Adult novels by Chris Crutcher and Gary Paulsen, for example, contain vivid sensory description on the first page.) Ask students, "What are your senses? To which of these does the description appeal? That is, does it help you see something? hear something? taste something?"

2. Elicit from students what a *still life* is (*painting or photograph of objects like flowers or fruit*). You may wish to display an example. Ask what they think a *verbal still life* might be (*a word-picture of an object or objects*).

3. Divide the class into groups of four or five and give each group a different fruit. Explain that they are going to observe the fruit carefully and describe their sensory impressions (how it looks, feels, smells, tastes, sounds).

4. Direct students to complete part A of **Handout 32** independently after group discussion. You may want to prompt groups by suggesting colorful language, e.g., *fuzzy* to describe the outer texture of a strawberry. Encourage specific impression words, too, e.g., *tangy, pungent, cloying*. A thesaurus may come in handy here.

5. Have students work individually on part B of the handout for five to ten minutes.

6. Have small groups share descriptive paragraphs. Direct each group to select one to be shared with the whole class. Conduct large group sharing. Instruct each group to share the paragraph without divulging the name of the object; see if others can guess.

7. Display an interesting scene portraying a group of people. Have students brainstorm dominant impressions of the picture—that is, the feelings captured by the picture and evoked from the viewer (serene, eerie, thoughtful, angry, playful). Record impressions on the board or overhead.

8. Have students brainstorm concrete sensory details based on the picture. Record these perceptions on the board or overhead.

9. Ask students to write short paragraphs describing the picture. Remind them to include both dominant impressions and specific sensory details. Encourage them to apply what they have learned about using comparison/contrast to develop their ideas.

10. Have volunteers share paragraphs orally.

The following is a sample scoring guide that might be used to guide students in writing their paragraph and to assess the finished products.

____ /5 Sensory details that appeal to at least four senses are included.

____ /5 The paragraph describes a dominant impression (feeling).

____ /5 A topic sentence is present.

____ /5 The paragraph contains at least five sentences that all describe the object.

____ /5 There are no errors in sentence structure (e.g., fragments, run-ons).

____ /5 There are no errors in G.U.M. (grammar, usage, mechanics).

____ /5 The paragraph contains colorful language with vivid, active verbs.

____ /35 Total points

Name _____

Date _____

Creating a Verbal Still Life

Part A.

Directions: After your group has been given its object, brainstorm some words and phrases that describe how the object looks, feels, smells, tastes, and sounds. Also, what are some "emotion" or "weather" words that describe your general impression of the object? Apply all of your senses in your examination. Be sure to consider both the object's outside and its inside. Fill in the chart below with specific, vivid words and phrases.

Object: _____

Category	Description
1. sight	
2. touch	
3. smell	
4. taste	
5. sound	
6. impressions	

Part B.

Directions: Artists sometimes paint *still lifes*, pictures of inanimate objects arranged to create specific impressions. On a separate sheet, compose a one-paragraph verbal still life describing your group's object. Include your dominant impression and relevant sense perceptions. Assume that your readers do *not* have the object in front of them.

Lesson 22
A Gallery of Descriptive Passages

Objective
• To examine descriptive techniques in a variety of literary passages

Notes to the Teacher
Although writers of all types tend to use description to support their main purposes, descriptive paragraphs are especially characteristic of narrative writing. The literary passages used as examples in this lesson are only a few of innumerable possibilities and can help assess students' aptitude for literary analysis. You may want to supplement with some of your favorites or with selections from students' previous or future literary study. Also, consider well-written newspaper articles and passages from high-interest Young Adult literature.

Procedure
1. Tell students that today's lesson will focus on literary descriptions by professional writers. Introduce the first passage on **Handout 33** by saying that Katherine Anne Porter has written a description of a grandmother. Ask students to imagine this old woman as they read. Have students read the first passage and respond to the questions.

Suggested Responses:

1. a. generally loving, generous, bright—but also stern, demanding, sometimes unjust

   b. "graceful confidence and a natural charmer"; "bountiful hospitality"; "victories of intelligence and feeling"; "flashes of perception"; "stern methodical disciplinarian"; "unjustly and ineffectively"

   c. admitting her age to herself; attempts at discipline; "spoiling" her children and grandchildren; reluctance to punish

2. Have partners complete the handout. Then review their responses.

Suggested Responses:

2. a. old, small, determined

   b. "walked slowly in the dark fine shadows"; "like the chirping of a solitary bird"; "numberless branching wrinkles"

   c. The first passage describes with generalizations and examples from first-hand knowledge; this one describes with images and figurative language from an objective observer.

3. a. busy, noisy, friendly, harmonious

   b. The street is compared to a harmonizing musical group.

   c. identifies diverse sounds that are part of the overall

4. a. a sailing vessel, The Narcissus, approaching harbor

   b. speed, grace, and beauty of the ship

   c. simile comparing ship to a great bird returning to nest; metaphors comparing/contrasting ship and clouds; personification of land, bays, other vessels

5. a. a glorious winter morning in the woods

   b. "frozen rime lusters the grass"; "pneumonia-making coldness"; "an ecstasy of shrillings"; "lemony sun pools"; "armada of speckled trout froths the water"

   c. sight, sound, touch, smell

6. a. timid, withdrawn, sick

   b. "sickly white hands"; "face was as white as his hands"; "cheeks were thin to hollowness"; "hair was dead and thin, almost feathery"; "a strange small spasm shook him"

   c. emphasizes his basic friendliness; negates malevolent undertones in passage

7. a. sight, touch

   b. He feels uncomfortable and out of place.

   c. Saturday morning, two weeks before New Year, Asian market in Houston, Danny's sense of culture clash

3. Students may have various responses to question 8. Use students' answers to generate a discussion of stylistic preferences, e.g., vivid sight images, effective similes, nature imagery, character portrayed, etc.

131

A Gallery of Descriptive Passages

Directions: Read the following descriptive passages. As you read, think about the questions that precede each passage. When you are done, answer the questions that follow the passage.

Passage 1

This excerpt is about the speaker's grandmother. As you read, ask yourself: What did this woman look and act like? How did the speaker feel about her?

> Grandmother had been an unusually attractive young woman, and she carried herself with the graceful confidence of a natural charmer to her last day. Her mirror did not deceive her, she saw that she was old. Her youthful confidence became matriarchal authority, a little way of knowing best about almost everything, of relying upon her own experience for sole guide, and I think now she had earned her power fairly. Her bountiful hospitality represented only one of her victories of intelligence and feeling over the stubborn difficulties of life. Her mind and her instinct ran in flashes of perception, and she sometimes had an airy, sharp, impatient way of speaking to those who didn't keep up with her. She believed it was her duty to be a stern methodical disciplinarian, and made a point of training us as she had been trained even to forbidding us to cross our knees, or to touch the back of our chair when we sat, or to speak until we were spoken to: love's labors lost utterly, for she had brought up a houseful of the worst spoiled children in seven counties, and started in again hopefully with a long series of motherless grandchildren—for the daughters of that afterwar generation did not survive so well as their mothers, they died in great numbers, leaving young husbands and children—who were to be the worst spoiled of any. She never punished anyone until she was exasperated beyond all endurance, when she was apt to let fly with a lightning, long-armed slap at the most unexpected moments, usually quite unjustly and ineffectually.
>
> —Katherine Anne Porter, "Portrait: Old South"

1. a. What is the speaker's overall impression of the grandmother? What words would she agree describe this old woman?

    b. Circle several words and phrases that express that impression.

    c. What supportive details does the speaker use to help build this "picture" of what the grandmother is like?

Passage 2

This excerpt is about an elderly woman who is walking across some frozen fields. As you read, try to picture her as she makes her way. Ask yourself: What kind of woman is this?

> It was December—a bright frozen day in the early morning. Far out in the country there was an old Negro woman with her head tied in a red rag, coming along a path through the pinewoods. Her name was Phoenix Jackson. She was very old and small and she walked slowly in the dark pine shadows, moving a little from side to side in her steps, with the balanced heaviness and lightness of a pendulum in a grandfather clock. She carried a thin, small cane made from an umbrella, and with this she kept tapping the frozen earth in front of her. This made a grave and persistent noise in the still air, that seemed meditative, like the chirping of a solitary little bird.
>
> She wore a dark striped dress reaching down to her shoetops, and an equally long apron of bleached sugar sacks, with a full pocket; all neat and tidy, but every time she took a step she might have fallen over her shoe-laces, which dragged from her unlaced shoes. She looked straight ahead. Her eyes were blue with age. Her skin had a pattern all its own of numberless branching wrinkles and as though a whole little tree stood in the middle of her forehead, but a golden color ran underneath, and the two knobs of her cheeks were illuminated by a yellow burning under the dark. Under the red rag her hair came down on her neck in the frailest of ringlets, still black, and with an odor like copper.
>
> —Eudora Welty, "A Worn Path"

2. a. What is your dominant impression of Phoenix Jackson?

   b. Circle some words and phrases that support that impression.

   c. Like the first passage, this one describes an elderly woman. How do the writers approach the task of creating their word-pictures of these women differently? How does the language, type of detail, and distance between the speaker and subject differ?

Passage 3

This excerpt is about a street in Philadelphia as it was in the past. As you read, try to run the scene like a movie through your head. Ask yourself: What do I see and hear? What is the speaker's perspective? How does he seem to feel about this place?

> But we can tell a good deal of what is going on along Chestnut Street without leaving our desk. Chestnut Street sings a music of its own. Its genial human sympathy could never be mistaken for that of any other highway. The various strands of sound that compose its harmony gradually sink into our mind without our paying conscious heed to them. For instance, there is the light sliding swish of the trolley poles along the wire, accompanied by the deep rocking rumble of the car, and the crash as it pounds over the cross-tracks at Sixth Street. There is the clear mellow clang of the trolley gongs, the musical trill of fast wagon wheels running along the trolley rails, and the rattle of hooves on the cobbled strip between the metals. Particularly easy to identify is the sound every citizen knows, the rasping, sliding clatter of a wagon turning off the car track so that a trolley can pass it. The front wheels have left the track, but the back pair are scraping along against the sets before mounting over the rim.
>
> — Christopher Morley, "Travel in Philadelphia"

3. a. Is this a positive or a negative picture? What words would you use to describe your impressions of what the street is like?

   b. What metaphor underlies the description? That is, to what is the writer comparing the street? How are they alike?

   c. How does the author develop the metaphor? That is, to which of the senses do most of the details appeal? How do these sensory details convey the idea that the street is like something else?

Passage 4

This excerpt describes a swift sailing ship called *The Narcissus*. As you read, try to picture the ship and the entire setting. Ask yourself: How does the speaker feel about this ship? How does the ship interact with its surroundings—Nature and other ships?

> Under white wings she skimmed low over the blue sea like a great bird speeding to its nest. The clouds raced with her mastheads; they rose astern enormous and white, soared to the zenith, flew past, and falling down the wide curve of the sky, seemed to dash headlong into the sea—the clouds swifter than the ship, more free, but without a home. The coast to welcome her stepped out of space into the sunshine. The lofty headlands trod masterfully into the sea; the wide bays smiled in the light; the shadows of homeless clouds ran along the sunny plains, leaped over valleys, without a check darted up the hills, rolled down the slopes; and the sunshine pursued them with patches of running brightness. On the brows of white cliffs white lighthouses shone in pillars of light. The Channel glittered like a blue mantle shot with gold and starred by the silver of the capping seas. The Narcissus rushed past the headlands and the bays. Outward-bound vessels crossed her track, lying over, and with their masts stripped for a slogging fight with the hard sou'wester. And, inshore, a string of smoking steamboats waddled, hugging the coast, like migrating and amphibious monsters, distrustful of the restless waves.
>
> —Joseph Conrad, *The Nigger of the Narcissus*

4. a. What exactly is the subject/action of this description?

   b. What qualities are emphasized in Conrad's description of the ship?

   c. Underline examples of imagery and figurative language used by Conrad to support his description.

Passage 5

This excerpt is about two people and a dog walking through the countryside. As you read, try to see, hear, and feel this scene as if you were on the walk. Ask yourself: How does the speaker feel about his companions and their walk?

> Morning. Frozen rime lusters the grass; the sun, round as an orange and orange as hot-weather moons, balances on the horizon, burnishes the silvered winter woods. A wild turkey calls. A renegade hog grunts in the undergrowth. Soon, by the edge of knee-deep, rapid-running water, we have to abandon the buggy. Queenie wades the stream first, paddles across barking complaints at the swiftness of the current, the pneumonia-making coldness of it. We follow, holding our shoes and equipment (a hatchet, a burlap sack) above our heads. A mile more: of chastising thorns, burrs and briars that catch at our clothes; of rusty pine needles brilliant with gaudy fungus and molted feathers. Here, there, a flash, a flutter, an ecstasy of shrillings remind us that not all the birds have flown south. Always, the path unwinds through lemony sun pools and pitch vine tunnels. Another creek to cross; a disturbed armada of speckled trout froths the water round us, and frogs the size of plates practice belly flops; beaver workmen are building a dam. On the farther shore, Queenie shakes herself and trembles. My friend shivers, too: not with cold but enthusiasm. One of her hat's ragged roses sheds a petal as she lifts her head and inhales the pine-heavy air. "We're almost there; can you smell it, Buddy?" she says, as though we were approaching an ocean.

—Truman Capote, *A Christmas Memory*

5. a. In one short phrase, summarize the writer's subject and the dominant impression conveyed.

   b. Underline at least three supportive details that convey how the morning looks, feels, or sounds.

   c. To what senses does Truman Capote appeal?

Passage 6

This excerpt describes a reclusive person who is seldom seen but often gossiped about. As you read, try to imagine him exactly as the speaker does. Ask yourself: What is he really like? How does the speaker feel toward him, during and after this encounter?

> He was still leaning against the wall. He had been leaning against the wall when I came into the room, his arms folded across his chest. As I pointed he brought his arms down and pressed the palms of his hands against the wall. They were white hands, sickly white hands that had never seen the sun, so white they stood out garishly against the dull cream wall in the dim light of Jem's room.
>
> I looked from his hands to his sand-stained khaki pants; my eyes traveled up his thin frame in his torn denim shirt. His face was as white as his hands, but for a shadow on his jutting chin. His cheeks were thin to hollowness; his mouth was wide; there were shallow, almost delicate indentations at his temples and his gray eyes were so colorless I thought he was blind. His hair was dead and thin, almost feathery on top of his head.
>
> When I pointed to him his palms slipped slightly, leaving greasy sweat streaks on the wall, and he hooked his thumbs in his belt. A strange small spasm shook him, as if he heard fingernails scrape slate, but as I gazed at him in wonder the tension slowly drained from his face. His lips parted into a timid smile.
>
> —Harper Lee, *To Kill a Mockingbird*

6. a. What is your general impression of the man described here? List three adjectives that you would use to describe him.

    b. Circle details in the passage that support that impression.

    c. Explain the importance of the last sentence in the passage. How might your impression of the man have been very different without that last sentence?

Passage 7

This excerpt is about a young man shopping with his mother. As you read, try to place yourself in the market. Ask yourself: What do I see, hear, and smell? How does the young man seem to feel about this place?

> Danny Vo jammed his hands into the pockets of his blue jeans, hoping no one from school would see him grocery shopping with his mother. But there was little chance of that. It was a late Saturday morning and only two weeks before what Americans called Chinese New Year, and what the Vietnamese called Tet. All the Asian shops clustered on Houston's Bellaire Boulevard bustled with customers. Up and down the narrow aisles of Di-Ho Market, women and children, and an occasional man, bumped elbows as they bought food for the upcoming stream of New Year's parties.
>
> Old women in baggy black pants lingered over the fruit and flower stands selecting ripe persimmons, small round winter melons, or fresh-cut gladiolus for the family ancestral altars. Children laughed and dashed around tables spilling over with neatly packaged plastic boxes of candied ginger, dried mandarin orange peel with licorice root, sweetened lotus seeds, fried melon seeds, and sugar-coated strips of coconut dyed pink, yellow, and green.
>
> —Sherry Garland, *Shadow of the Dragon*

7. a. The author has chosen many specific details in describing this scene. As you imagine the scene, which senses do you use and which details do you find most vivid?

   b. What is your impression of Danny Vo and his place in this scene?

   c. Setting includes time, place, and social setting. How does this passage describe all three of these aspects?

8. All of these descriptions work well, yet they differ greatly in topic, impression, style, and type of detail.

   a. Which passage would you select as your favorite of the seven?

   b. Why?

   c. What is one line from your favorite description that you wish you had written?

Lesson 23
A Description Portfolio

Objective
- To execute a project for an original description portfolio

Notes to the Teacher
Art students are familiar with the use of a portfolio, a collection of significant pieces representing their best work. In this lesson, a similar approach prompts students to compose a collection of descriptions, some or all of which may later be useful in extended writings.

The project described here challenges students to structure their own prewriting experiences as observers. You may want to caution students to use prudence in selecting an observation site; it is sometimes advisable to suggest traveling in pairs.

Before this lesson, privately ask two or three students to spend the first ten minutes carefully observing someone in the classroom and recording descriptions of his or her appearance, mannerisms, reactions, interactions, etc. Select student observers who are fundamentally friendly toward the others in the class. Make it clear that the observers will be sharing their notes; if there is a potential for a certain written observation—no matter how accurate—to cause anyone embarrassment, it should be omitted.

Note: Kathleen Blake Yancey has compiled a fascinating, informative collection of essays using portfolios called *Portfolios in the Writing Classroom* (NCTE, 1992).

Procedure
1. Write the word *portfolio* on the board (and if you have an art portfolio, hold it up in front of the class). Discuss what a portfolio is. (*It is a portable case for holding loose papers; in the writing classroom, it has come to mean a collection of writings done over a period of time.*) Also discuss what it is used for. (*For one thing, a portfolio gives not only the teacher, but students themselves, an opportunity to see growth.*) Explain that in this lesson, students will be planning and carrying out a project leading to a portfolio of descriptive writings.

2. Have students read **Handout 34**, and take time to clarify directions and answer questions.

3. Explain that several students have, during the last few minutes, had a little practice in observing and recording descriptive details. If (and only if) the person who was observed by the volunteer gives permission, ask one of the observers to share his or her observations and record the observations on the board. Use specific examples to show how careful observation can yield colorful details that a writer might have trouble generating through imagination alone. Repeat this procedure with the other two student observers.

4. If desired, have students read and discuss William Wordsworth's "I wandered lonely as a cloud" as a poetic example of observation and imagination leading to writing.

5. On the day students bring portfolios to class:

   - Have students select three favorite descriptions from their portfolios, and code them with a star or some other symbol.

   - Direct small groups of four to five to share these starred descriptions and to reach a consensus on each person's most successful passage. Have students code these descriptions with multiple stars or other symbols.

   - Ask each group to select one passage to be shared with the class. If the passage is in a computer file or can be photocopied, it is easy to create a transparency for the overhead projector. Otherwise, the group can share orally. Encourage comments on particularly effective details and phrases.

   - Have students write a short letter of introduction to their description portfolio. In the letter, they should give their readers an overview of the ten pieces. They should point out at least one success they had in writing each piece. They should then reflect on how they improved as writers during the process of composing their portfolio.

6. A portfolio checklist like the following might be used to score and assess students' ability to plan and carry out their tasks.

_____ Ten descriptions are written, each on a separate paper or index card.

_____ Feedback summaries are included for each piece.

_____ The three favorite descriptions are starred.

_____ The group has coded what they agree to be each person's most successful piece.

_____ The writer has included a letter of introduction to the portfolio.

Name _____

Date _____

Planning a Description Portfolio

Directions: Complete the following steps as directed to create a portfolio of descriptive writing.

1. Choose a situation in which you can be an observer, perceiving many details of the changing scene around you for at least an hour. You will, in a sense, place a magic circle around yourself, separating yourself from the people and things you observe. You might choose a seat on a city bus, the school cafeteria, a shopping mall, an airport terminal, a zoo, a place in the woods, or any other location for observation and description that appeals to you.

    Observation place: _____

    Time(s): _____

2. Once you have situated yourself, notice that you can focus your observation on objects, individual people, and group interactions. For example, in a mall you might observe an old man dozing on a bench in front of a fountain, a shoplifter dodging department store security guards, and a toy store's window display. The possibilities are endless!

3. Select ten observations and record impressions and details to be used later in composing descriptions. Be sure that your notes include the subtle nuances and surprising incongruities of real life.

Observation	Impression	Details
1.		
2.		
3.		
4.		

Observation	Impression	Details
5.		
6.		
7.		
8.		
9.		
10.		

4. Use your notes, memories, and imagination to compose ten descriptions of objects, people and interactions, and events. Ask one or more people to be readers and responders. Use a feedback summary form like **Handout 29** to record their comments. Consider their suggestions before your finalize the descriptions. Staple together revisions and earlier drafts, with the latest draft on top in each case. Add an introductory letter to your readers giving an introduction to the ten pieces. Put them in a description portfolio (each passage on a separate paper or index card). Decorate the portfolio, if you like, and bring it to class.

Part 6
Persuasion/Argumentation

In both persuasion and argumentation, the writer attempts to move the audience from one point to another. They differ in their degrees of emphasis on logic. Persuasion makes use of emotional appeals and psychology to prompt the reader to do something; one example is the advertising industry, with its programs to motivate us to buy or invest. The argument, on the other hand, stresses the use of logic to convince the audience of a specific idea. In practice, persuasion and argumentation are often intermingled.

The lessons in this section lead students to several short compositions and an extended argument. Schedule ample drafting time between Lessons 29 and 30, as well as revision and editing time after Lesson 30.

Lesson 24
The World of Advertising

Objectives
- To analyze persuasive writing through a study of advertisements
- To demonstrate how the persuasive writer's awareness of purpose and audience shapes the written product

Notes to the Teacher

Advertisements affect all of us daily, attempting to persuade us to spend, invest, or donate money or time. Students themselves are familiar with ads that appeal to desires to avoid acne, smell good, and be in the popular group. This lesson examines the advertisement as a form of persuasive writing. Students focus on the advertisement writer's intense awareness of purpose and audience as key factors shaping the written product. Their responses to **Handout 35** can be used to assess their abilities to analyze persuasive writing.

To begin the lesson, you will need a large, effective, and colorful magazine advertisement.

Procedure

1. Post the magazine advertisement on the board or a bulletin board and ask students to examine it. Ask: "What is the ad's purpose?" (*to persuade the audience to buy the product*) "How does this ad attempt to persuade you to buy the product? How successful is it? Why?" Try to elicit from students that advertising combines the skills of the writer and the graphic artist in a joint effort to persuade an audience. Point out that this lesson will focus on the writer's role as students examine advertising copy.

2. Distribute **Handout 35** and have students complete part A.

   Suggested Responses:

   1. *to persuade the reader to buy a Subaru, or at least to consider its value*

   2. *The writer assumes that the reader is concerned with safety on the road, especially during bad weather; has a desire for an economical car; and is a middle-aged adult driver.*

3. *safety through four-wheel drive; "state-of-the-art" developments; reasonable costs; popular vehicle*

   4. *The phrase "four-wheel drive" is repeated to emphasize the safety benefit of this feature and to make it stick in the consumer's mind.*

   5. *"number one four-wheel drive car in America," i.e., there is a large group of American buyers*

   6. *Some students may note that this car does not sound very exciting.*

3. Ask students where they think this ad might be printed. (*Ads like it appear in weekly magazines such as* Time *and* Newsweek.) Ask whether it would be effective in a magazine geared primarily toward a teen audience. Lead students to recognize that advertisers often assume teens are less concerned with safety features and durability of a product than older consumers are. An ad aimed at teens is more likely to stress the social benefits and fun associated with owning a Subaru.

4. Stress that advertisements usually attempt to sell something. To succeed, the copy writer needs an intense awareness of both purpose and target audience.

5. Have students complete part B.

   Suggested Responses:

   1. *"cooking for your celeb crush," "win a humongous slumber party," "Entering is as fun 'n' easy as making a . . . cookie," "trendy messenger bag," "cool CD"*

   2. *to encourage the purchase of Pillsbury cookie dough and associate the Pillsbury brand name with having a good time*

      anyone who enjoys making cookies and winning contests—especially teenage girls

   3. *uses a "we are your friends" tone toward teens: "for your celeb crush," "Helpful hint," "Once you've whipped up an idea."*

4. *desires for sweet treats, fun, freebies; interest in celebrities*

5. *Ads to an older audience often appeal to security, to the desire to stay young, to the desire to seem powerful or wealthy.*

6. Have students complete part C.

   Suggested Responses:

   1. *to solicit enlistments in the army*

   2. *high school juniors and seniors who plan to go to college; college freshmen*

   3. *The writer assumes that the audience has a need for financial help; desire for adventure; a concern with physical fitness; and a desire to mature in perspective.*

   4. *specific amounts of money for college; travel opportunities, outstanding physical fitness; knowledge about the world; self-knowledge*

   5. *Possible answers:*

      a. *Does a recruit have to do anything to qualify for the Army College Fund? (e.g., get a high school diploma within a certain period, get certain test scores)?*

      b. *Exactly what are the specialties, and how do I qualify for them?*

      c. *After I leave the military, how is the college money I earned paid to me? Are there any restrictions on how long I have to enter a program—or what education program I enter?*

7. Point out that the Army ad recognizes that people can respond from a variety of needs and motivations. Explain that Abraham Maslow (1903–1970), an American psychologist and expert on human motivation, conceptualized human needs in a hierarchy (a series of steps) with needs on lower levels having to be met before the individual could rise to the next level. Have students try to predict what needs he included. As they brainstorm their predictions, jot these suggestions on the board. Then share Maslow's hierarchy:

5. Self-actualization Needs (appreciation for beauty, creativity, humor)

4. Self-esteem Needs (leadership, competence, intelligence)

3. Love Needs (affection, belonging, participation)

2. Safety Needs (security, comfort, order, protection)

1. Physical Needs (oxygen, water, food, sleep, exercise)

Take a few minutes to discuss with students how these needs are satisfied in their lives. For example, what opportunities do they have to fulfill their need for creativity? Which needs are usually met completely? Which ones are not?

Advertisements are a form of propaganda (biased information). Advertisers not only try to convince consumers that a product fulfills existing needs, they also try to create new needs. See if students can think of examples among commonly shown TV ads. For extra credit, you might have students take notes on a few TV ads, then analyze the wording of one of the more effective ones. Whom does it try to persuade? What does it try to persuade consumers who are in that group? How?

Explain that Maslow gave the name *self-actualization* to the stage of development at which a person utilizes his or her potential to become all that he or she is capable of being.

Point out that the Army advertisement addresses almost all of the need levels, thus appealing to a variety of people. Point out, too, that the Army ad does not address the need for safety/security. It does not reassure recruits about their personal safety; in fact, it does not mention the potential for armed conflict at all. Why not?

8. Have small groups complete **Handout 36**.

   Suggested Responses:

   1. Phillips 66

   Purpose—*ambiguous; to create a good image; perhaps to attract investors, to get donations for research or to sell Phillips 66 products*

   Target audience—*conservationists; bird lovers; patriots*

   Needs/desires addressed—*growth needs; identification with a good cause; love for national symbol; hint at threat to safety/security*

   2. Kellogg's Raisin Bran

   Purpose—*to persuade people to buy Kellogg's Raisin Bran*

   Target audience—*parents with young children*

   Needs/desires addressed—*parents' need/desire to express love for children by satisfying children's physiological needs*

   3. Northwest

   Purpose—*to solicit participants in Northwest's Asia tours*

   Target audience—*people attracted by exotic images of Far East; wealthy travelers who prefer security and comfort*

   Needs/desires addressed—*desire to travel; attraction to Asian culture; safety/security; comfort*

9. Ask students to revise one of the ads from **Handout 35** for a different purpose and/or audience. For example, how might the car ad differ if it were aimed at twentysomethings? What if the pickle people decided that middle-aged dieters were an untapped market? How might the wording of the ad change if the Army were trying to recruit more people with high-tech skills?

The following scoring guide can be used to evaluate finished advertisements.

___ /5   Clear audience

___ /5   Clear purpose

___ /5   appeals to at least two needs

___ /5   strong persuasive language

___ /20   Total points

147

The Writer's World of Advertising

Part A.

Directions: When we think of writers, we seldom think of those who compose copy for advertisements. Yet, of all writers, they may have the most readers per written word! Read the ad for Subaru and answer the questions that follow.

Subaru 4 Wheel Drive Keeps a Car
From Becoming an Off Road Vehicle

Subaru Four Wheel Drive is designed to keep you on the road, regardless of the conditions. In fact, we feel so strongly about the traction it gives, we offer four wheel drive on virtually every car we build. So there's no reason to think of it as something found only on trucks.

And over the years, we've offered everything from "on demand" four wheel drive system to a new state-of-the-art full time four wheel drive system.

What's more, Subaru with four wheel drive is reasonable to buy, maintain and operate. Not to mention, Subaru is the number one four wheel drive car in America. Subaru, the car that keeps hazardous road conditions from turning into hazardous driving conditions. Subaru.

1. What is the writer's main purpose?

2. What does the ad writer seem to assume about the reader?

3. What does the writer offer the reader?

4. How and why does the ad writer use repetition?

5. Where does the ad suggest that you will belong to a good group if you buy this car?

6. Does the ad's wording appeal to you? Why or why not?

7. Find the one phrase in the ad that you feel is the most strongly persuasive, and write it below.

Part B.

Directions: Read the ad, and answer the questions.

Pillsbury presents: Cooking for your celeb crush sweeps

Win a humongous slumber party for you and 20 of your friends! Entering is as fun 'n' easy as making a Pillsbury OneStep Cookie. Just tell us which celebrity you'd bake a OneStep Cookie for and how you'd decorate it. Helpful hint: You can cut it in different shapes, top it with icing or frosting, or put your favorite topping on it. The options are endless!

1 Grand Prize Winner

- An all-expense paid slumber party for you and 20 of your friends.
- A sleek messenger bag, cool CD and a night's worth of free cookies for each of your guests (and yourself, of course!)

100 First Place Winners

- Trendy messenger bag and a cool CD

3000 Second Place Winners

- Cool CD

1. List words and phrases in the Pillsbury ad which would appeal to a teenage audience.

2. What is the purpose of the ad?

3. Describe the tone of the ad.

4. What desires are used as an appeal?

5. Can you think of an ad that appeals to an older audience? What different desires are used to attract more mature readers?

Part C.

Directions: Examine the ad and answer the questions that follow.

Joining the Army May Be the Smartest Thing You Can Do for Your College Education

With the G.I. Bill plus the Army College Fund, you can earn up to $40,000 for college while you serve. Here's how:

You contribute $100 per month toward your education during the first year of service. All you contribute is $12,000.00. Then the government—through the GI Bill plus the Army College Fund—can provide up to $40,000 for a four-year enlistment. (For a three-year enlistment, the government can provide up to $33,000 and for a two-year enlistment, up to $26,500.)

Of course, how much you earn depends on how long you serve and which specialty you qualify and enlist for.

But you'll get a lot more out of your enlistment than the money you can earn for college.

Other Benefits Are Hard to Beat

1. Travel and adventure.
2. Meeting new people.
3. Getting into the best physical shape you've ever been in.
4. No cost or low cost medical and dental care.
5. 30 days of paid vacation earned each year.
6. Outstanding sports and recreational facilities.
7. Movies, arts & crafts and other leisure-time activities.

If you'd like to learn more about the G.I. Bill plus the Army College Fund, visit your local Army Recruiter. Or call, toll free, 1-800-USA-ARMY.

Army. Be All You Can Be.

1. What is the writer's main purpose?

2. Who is the target audience?

3. What does the writer assume about the audience?

4. What offers does the advertisement include?

5. What questions does the ad not answer about getting money for college by enlistment? List at least three questions a potential recruit would need to ask in order to evaluate just how good a deal this is.

   a.

   b.

   c.

Contrasting Advertisements

Directions: Examine the following ads for an oil company, a cereal company, and an airline. Consider the similarities of and differences between the three ads' purposes, target audiences, and appeals. Write down your ideas in the chart.

The Eagle Has Landed

In Oklahoma and Mississippi, Georgia and Alabama. Where few bald eagle nests have produced young in the last 50 years. Using precious eggs and dedicated effort, the Sutton Avian Research Center is successfully raising eagles from fuzzy to fierce. And releasing them into the skies bald eagles once called home. Phillips Petroleum supports this unique program to re-establish our endangered national symbol.

After all, if Man can land an Eagle on the moon, he can surely keep them landing on the earth.

Phillips 66

For more information, contact the George Miksch Sutton Avian Research Center, Inc., P.O. Box 2007, Bartlesville, OK 74005 (918) 336–7778.

Kids Need Fiber, and Raisins

Fiber is important for everyone—even kids. But how often do your kids ask for fiber? They want something that tastes good.

That's why *Kellogg's* packs its Raisin Bran with *two scoops* of raisins. So your kids get the fiber they need with a taste they love. (100% of the U.S. RDA of iron, too!) Delicious *Kellogg's* Raisin Bran. It's fiber kids love.

Kellogg's

Asia. The Way You Always Dreamed It Would Be.

Emerald Buddhas. Floating markets. The Stone Forest. The Land of Smiles. A tour of the Far East will dazzle your senses like no dream.

Choose from a host of deluxe escorted tours to China. We also offer escorted and independent tours of Thailand, Japan, Korea, and even Bali. Complete air/land packages to Bangkok begin at just $1,099.

And behind every tour, you'll find Northwest's 40 years of experience to Asia. Plus comforts no other U.S. airline offers you—like a spacious 747 on every flight.

So if you're looking for the experience of a lifetime, look to the airline with a lifetime of experience. Northwest, the number one airline to Asia. Call your travel agent or Northwest at (800)NWA-TOUR.

Look To Us.
Northwest

Ad	Purpose	Target Audience	Needs/ Desires Addressed
1. Phillips 66			
2. Kellogg's Raisin Bran			
3. Northwest			

Lesson 25
Group Advertisements

Objective
- To create advertisements

Notes to the Teacher
This lesson teaches students to compose advertisements for unusual products. Ad copy introduces students to the essence of persuasive writing—targeting an audience, pointing out or creating a need, emphasizing the idea or product's merits, and spurring an action. No matter how bizarre the product, the copy must still concentrate on the reader's own interests. A good ad for a pet peanut, for example, might address the need most of us have for steady companionship.

Use this lesson not as a formal, graded exercise in advertising, but as a creative introduction to persuasive techniques and an assessment of students' familiarity with them.

Procedure
1. Have students share in pairs or groups the rewritten ads they created in Lesson 24.

2. Have students brainstorm a list of products to advertise. Encourage out-of-the-ordinary products, like a pet peanut (leash included), musical water-skis, perforated egg shells, or an action movie starring two scoops of strawberry ice cream. Such products will force students to consider how to manipulate the reader's interests.

3. Have students consider some unusual target markets for one or two of these items. These should be groups that an ad writer might find it challenging to convince that they need the product. For example, it would be difficult to sell musical water-skis to a desert dweller.

4. Divide the class into small groups. Have them choose a scribe to record the group's responses. Then have them select a product and audience and answer questions 1 and 2 on **Handout 37**.

5. Explain that advertising companies thoroughly know their product. They highlight its advantages and minimize or disguise its liabilities. For example, the cereal ad analyzed in the previous lesson does not mention that the cereal is relatively high in calories and the Army ad minimizes the factors that can make a recruit ineligible for some of the money by making a general statement that "how much you earn depends on how long you serve and which specialty you qualify and enlist for." Have students discuss and answer questions 3 and 4 as completely as possible.

6. Review Maslow's need hierarchy. Perhaps display the "steps" on a piece of poster board or on the overhead. Have students answer questions 5 and 6.

7. Give students time to draft their advertisement copy and attach a finished copy to the handout. If time permits, have students illustrate and display their ads.

8. The following can be used as a scoring guide for student advertisements:

   _____ /5   A product is named.

   _____ /5   The audience is clear.

   _____ /5   At least three colorful words are used to describe product.

   _____ /5   The ad appeals to—or creates— at least one need.

   _____ /5   The ad highlights advantages.

   _____ /5   The ad minimizes or ignores disadvantages.

   _____ /10   The ad is creative, persuasive, appealing.

   _____ /40   Total points

Creating an Ad

Directions: Work with your group to make an advertisement for something wild and wacky. Choose a scribe to record the group's responses to the items below, and create the advertisement as directed.

1. What is your product?

2. Who is your target audience?

3. What are the positive features of your product? What is so good about it? What problem does it solve? How does it make life easier or better?

4. What are the negative features of your product? These are things like high cost or poor quality that you will minimize or not mention in your ad.

5. What needs, both practical and psychological, will this product satisfy? Will it make the consumer healthier? happier? more attractive?

6. Does this ad assume that the consumer has a certain fear? Does it try to create a certain fear that the consumer may not have already had? If so, what fear(s)?

7. Draft your advertising copy. Use the following frame, if you like.

   Attention all of you _____ out there! Isn't it time you bought a _____?

   They're _____ (strong describing word). Plus they're _____.

   And they're _____. You'll never need to _____ again! Think

   of it! No more _____ and no more _____.

   Unlike our competitors, we _____. Buy a _____ today!

8. Revise and edit your draft. Staple the finished copy this handout.

Lesson 26
The Persuasive Letter

Objective
- To apply guidelines for effective persuasion in a letter-writing context

Notes to the Teacher
Advertising's intense focus on purpose and audience also characterizes other forms of persuasive writing. Whether in a letter ("Please refund my money.") or an article ("Vote for X"), persuasion aims to motivate an audience to do something.

"You draw more flies with honey than with vinegar," states an old adage. The materials in this lesson emphasize that courtesy and respect usually generate a more positive response than coercion or threats. By examining three letters of varying quality, students learn to apply guidelines for effective persuasion.

Procedure
1. Read students an effective letter of persuasion. These are often found among the letters to the editor in the newspaper. There are also some very funny, effective letters of complaint reprinted in *Letters of a Nation*, edited by Andrew Carroll, (Kodansha America, Inc., 1997).

2. Tell students that strategies for effective advertising are also useful in situations where one person wants to persuade another to do something. Point out that focus on purpose and awareness of audience are key factors.

3. Have students complete **Handout 38**, part A.

   Suggested Responses:
   1. a. purpose—*to persuade Pete to come home for Susan's prom*

      b. audience—*Pete, Susan's boyfriend, a college freshman*

   2. *The first letter scolds, accuses, complains, suggests threat of competition, orders, treats him as relatively unimportant, and threatens.*

   3. *The second letter appeals to the need for affection and understanding; the desire to care for another; the desire to have fun; the need for respect; the desire for a car.*

   4. *The second is more likely to bring Pete home for prom, since it gives a variety of strong, positive reasons; the first suggests an irritating experience with a selfish, complaining person.*

4. List on the board or overhead four guidelines for effective persuasion; add comments to clarify each point.

   a. Use a positive, courteous approach.
      - "You draw more flies with honey than with vinegar."
      - Even when we allow force to motivate us, we tend to feel resentful and uncooperative.

   b. Appeal to a variety of needs and desires.
      - Most human actions are shaped by a combination of motivations, not just by one.

   c. Clearly state what you want your audience to do.
      - Otherwise confusion results.

   d. Clearly state what your next step in communication will be.
      - "I will call you within the next few days."

5. Have students complete part B.

   Suggested Responses:
   1. *Yes—affirmation of Smith as a businessman and citizen; no blame or threats*

   2. *appeals to desire to please customers, interest in community needs, Thanksgiving spirit, awareness of weakened economy, need for advertising*

   3. *first two sentences of paragraph 5*

   4. *phone call on a specific day, or Smith's return call at his convenience*

   5. *Use students' answers to generate a general discussion of subjective reactions to various appeals. That is, we receive written requests in many forms: letters, e-mails, newsletters, public notices, etc.*

*What distinguishes an effective one—
one to which we are more likely to
respond positively—from one that is not?*

6. Point out that persuasive letters can be used in a variety of contexts. Ask students to brainstorm possible topics. Stimulate ideas by suggesting some of these:

    a. to persuade a company to return your money for an unsatisfactory product

    b. to persuade your parents to send you more money at school or camp

    c. to persuade a political figure or entertainer to speak at a school assembly

    d. to persuade someone to interview you for a job opening

    e. to persuade the state government or school board to change a ruling, e.g., to drop turnpike tolls or restore funding for an educational program

    f. to persuade a company to send you free samples

    g. to persuade naturalists to classify the dandelion as a wildflower rather than a weed.

    h. to persuade a friend to join you on a camping trip

    i. to persuade a college admissions officer that you have something to offer that school

    j. to persuade an organization to let you volunteer for them

    k. to persuade the_____ Association that you deserve one of its scholarships

7. Ask students to write persuasive letters. Direct them to seek conferencing from someone similar to the target audience: e.g., a parent if the audience is a business; a teacher if the audience is the school administration. Assign a reasonable date for revised, edited letters to be submitted.

The Art of Persuasion

Part A.

Directions: Read these two letters carefully. Then answer the questions that follow.

Letter 1

May 3, 2000

Dear Pete,

I can't believe you're not planning to come home for the prom weekend. You couldn't possibly have so much work to do that you can't take a little time off for my sake. After all, I'm still stuck in high school, while you're off having a great time in college.

I'm sick and tired of boring weekends babysitting. Steve King asked me out this Saturday, and I think I will go. You don't mind, do you? He's like a brother to me. Did I tell you that he asked me to go to the prom with him?

Please make arrangements to be here May 10. The prom goes from 8:00 to midnight. There are a lot of parties afterwards. They're nothing special, but I don't want to miss them. Cedar Point is Sunday, but you don't have to go to that. I'll go with Connie and Jill. That way you can catch the early Greyhound back to school.

I'm in charge of one of the prom committees, and after all the work I've done, I think I deserve to be there. Don't you think you owe me that much? Don't call this weekend unless your answer is YES. I'll be too angry to talk to you at all if you decide not to come.

Susan

Letter 2

May 3, 2000

Dear Pete,

I've been thinking about you a lot since you called last Saturday. You sounded tired and a little down, and I wished I could be there to cheer you up! It's too bad you had to graduate a year ahead of me, and beat me to ND. I imagine you've been studying too much and playing not enough. Is that calculus course still awful?

I've been missing you a lot. The weekends aren't much fun except when you're home. The only good thing is that I've made quite a bit of money babysitting and doing odd jobs.

I know you weren't planning to come home again until after final exams. But I was wondering if maybe you might change your mind and come for the prom weekend May 10. The prom is Friday from 8:00 to midnight, and a whole series of activities follows, ending with a trip to Cedar Point on Sunday. You'd have a lot of fun and we'd be together.

My brother Dan said he'd loan you his Buick so you can drive straight from Cedar Point back to school. (I'll get a ride home with Connie and Jill—their dates have to work Sunday.) Dan said you can keep the car until you come home after exams.

This afternoon we have a meeting of the prom planning committee (PPC, for short). I'm in charge of decorations and favors, and we've come up with some really clever ideas. I won't tell you about them now, since I'm hoping you'll be there in person to see them! Looking forward to talking to you on the phone this weekend.

Love,
Susan

1. These two letters have the same purpose and audience. Identify them.

   a. purpose

   b. audience

2. How does the first letter appeal to Pete's needs and desires?

3. What approach does the second letter use?

4. Which letter is more likely to bring Pete home for Susan's prom? Explain your choice.

Part B.

Directions: Carefully read this letter and answer the questions that follow.

9105 Service Lane
Lincoln, MD 20854

October 10, 2000

Albert Smith, Owner
Smith's Grocery
17 Cornucopia Way
Lincoln, MD 20854

Dear Mr. Smith:

Smith's Grocery has always been considered one of the finest food stores in town. My parents, as well as most of our neighbors, prefer your store for its fresh produce, well-trimmed meats, reasonable prices, and pleasant environment.

Besides having a superior grocery, you have also contributed generously to our community. Last year you helped the Lincoln High School band in its campaign to purchase new uniforms. Two years ago you personally led an outstanding, successful drive for the Cystic Fibrosis Fund.

Can you help us this year? Our Key Club has discovered that there are, in our own community, families unable to provide sufficient food for their children. We would like to help them.

The Thanksgiving season is only a month away, and our goal is to provide a full, nourishing holiday dinner for ten needy families recommended by the Clergy Council. All of these families were seriously hurt by the collapse of the steel industry eight years ago.

We are asking you to donate the meat and vegetables for the Thanksgiving dinners. This would include turkeys, potatoes, green beans, and celery. Our Key Club treasury will purchase bread, milk, and pumpkin pies for the rest of the meal. We will also prepare and personally deliver the food.

Our local Channel 5 plans to feature this project in the evening news during the second week of November. If you are interested in helping us, the camera crew would like to do some taping at Smith's Grocery on November 4, including a short interview with you.

I will call you on Monday, October 28, to discuss your ideas about our project. Meanwhile, if you have any questions or comments, please contact me through the Lincoln High School Guidance Office.

Thank you for your time and interest.

Sincerely,

Jim Kelly

Jim Kelly
President, Lincoln High School Key Club

1. Does this letter use a positive courteous approach? Find specific evidence to support your answer.

2. Find examples of different approaches Jim Kelly uses to appeal to Albert Smith.

3. Where does Kelly state exactly what he wants Smith to do?

4. What future communication steps are suggested?

5. Do you think Smith is likely to respond positively to Kelly's request? Explain your answer.

6. Is there anything you think Kelly should have added or taken out?

Lesson 27
Analogies

Objectives
- To recognize how analogies are used
- To write analogies

Notes to the Teacher

Although the argumentative essay rises and falls on its logic, images help to clarify ideas and persuade the reader. The best argumentative essays contain sound logic to convince the left brain, and appealing images to satisfy the right brain. Students are already familiar with the power of images in advertising and television. Many of these images are created by apt analogy—a comparison of two things alike in certain aspects.

In exposition and description, analogy is a method by which an unfamiliar object or idea is explained or described by comparing it with objects or ideas that are probably more familiar to the reader. A good popular science writer, for example, often explains scientific abstractions by comparing them with everyday objects and processes. Literary writers, too, use similes (expressed analogies) and metaphors (implied ones).

Analogies usually function to clarify a point, not to present new evidence. The things compared have at least one similarity—but are not alike in every way. To understand what the analogy means, the reader needs to be able to identify that similarity. "Life is a rollercoaster ride" refers to life's ups and downs, not to the fact that you are required to wear a restraint. This analogy is apt because it captures one aspect of life well (its ups and downs); however, like any analogy, it does not capture other facets (such as our freedom to change tracks). Some analogies do not work at all because they are founded on faulty reasoning, which a good critical reader learns to detect. Class discussion and handout work will allow students to develop a critical faculty for analogies.

Procedure

1. Write the word *analogy* on the board or overhead along with a good example—from today's newspaper, perhaps. For example, a sportswriter criticizing the manager of a losing baseball team: "Inspirational leadership is largely smoke and mirrors. You have to fool 'em into thinking you've got magic. He has been out of tricks for months."

2. Elicit from students what an analogy is. Have them analyze what two things are compared in your example, and how they are alike. (*The manager is like a magician who is out of tricks; neither can fool anyone and both, therefore, lose their reputations.*) Supply the key information from Notes to the Teacher.

3. Have students brainstorm examples of common analogies (*hard as nails, sly as a fox, quick as a flash*). See if students can come up with examples. Point out, too, that many of the mythical allusions that have made it into everyday language are analogies. Have students brainstorm and analyze a few of these. (*Doing that really opens up a Pandora's box. He made a herculean effort to finish the project on time. That problematic situation is her Scylla and Charybis.*)

4. Collect the persuasive letters students wrote in Lesson 26, or have students read them in groups. Strictly speaking, this is not a conference, but a sharing. Students should not be given time to revise and edit at this point.

5. Have students complete **Handout 39**.

   Suggested Responses:

   1. *the expansion of the universe*
   2. *a balloon with dots*
   3. *As in the universe, the space between the dots (galaxies) is expanding. As with galaxies, from one dot all the other dots seem to be receding.*
   4. *Unlike the universe, which is three-dimensional, the balloon surface is only two-dimensional. Unlike the galaxies, which do not expand, the balloon dots do expand.*

6. Chose any prominent person—living, dead, fictional, even yourself—and have the class brainstorm that person's qualities. Then have students create analogies to illustrate different qualities. The goal is to have one analogy explain as many different characteristics as possible.

Example:

Mr. Jones

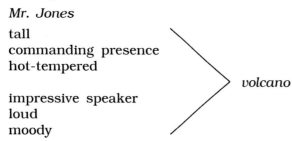

tall
commanding presence
hot-tempered

impressive speaker
loud
moody

volcano

Another method might be to take any object, brainstorm or cluster characteristics or associations, and then decide what person this object describes.

7. Brainstorm more complex, concrete subjects for analogies (*school, work, sports, clubs, government, television*). Select one, and have students list characteristics about that subject and devise analogies.

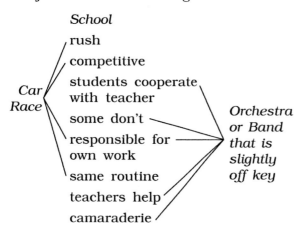

School

rush
competitive
students cooperate with teacher
some don't
responsible for own work
same routine
teachers help
camaraderie

Car Race

Orchestra or Band that is slightly off key

Analogies may and should overlap. Encourage different analogies for the same characteristics. Then discuss ways the analogy is dissimilar to its subject.

8. Brainstorm abstract ideas for analogies (*love, friendship, honor, truth*). Select one, and have students list characteristics and analogies.

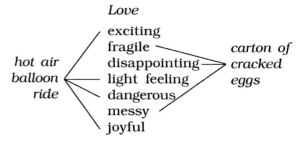

Love

exciting
fragile
disappointing
light feeling
dangerous
messy
joyful

hot air balloon ride

carton of cracked eggs

You might again cluster objects and see if those descriptions apply to any abstract ideas.

9. Have students complete **Handout 40**.

Optional Activity

Have students look through newspapers and magazines for opinions and advertisements that are based on faulty analogies. Campaign ads are rich sources of these. Have students analyze what two things are being compared, and explain why that comparison does not really work. Emphasize that too often people are persuaded by arguments that rest on faulty analogies, so they should always regard analogies with a critical eye.

The Figurative and Functional Analogy

Directions: Read the information about analogies below. Then read the passage and answer the four questions that follow.

Tim's as tall as a flagpole.

How are Tim and a flagpole alike? Both are tall. This simile emphasizes Tim's height.

That car is a lemon.

How is the car like a lemon? Both leave a sour taste in your mouth. This metaphor emphasizes the car's imperfection.

These figures of speech add color and detail to our writing. When we use them to explain a point, in expository essays, they are called *analogies*. Analogies use a familiar subject to explain or clarify a less familiar subject or idea. For example, if you were explaining word processors to an older person unacquainted with them, you might compare them to typewriters. When Abraham Lincoln wanted to explain government—a very complex idea—he used a familiar object: "A house divided against itself cannot stand." *Similes* and *metaphors* are two types of analogies.

Look for the analogy in this passage:

> My nonmathematical friends often tell me that they find it difficult to picture this expansion. Short of using a lot of mathematics I cannot do better than use the analogy of a balloon with a large number of dots marked on its surface. If the balloon is blown up, the distances between the dots increase in the same way as the distances between the galaxies. Here I should give a warning that this analogy must not be taken too strictly. There are several important respects in which it is definitely misleading. For example, the dots on the surface of a balloon would themselves increase in size as the balloon was being blown up. This is not the case for the galaxies, for their internal gravitational fields are sufficiently strong to prevent any such expansion. A further weakness of our analogy is that the surface of an ordinary balloon is two dimensional—that is to say, the points of its surface can be described by two co-ordinates; for example, by latitude and longitude. In the case of the Universe we must think of the surface as possessing a third dimension. This is not as difficult as it may sound. We are all familiar with pictures in perspective—pictures in which artists have represented three-dimensional scenes on two-dimensional canvases. So it is not really a difficult conception to imagine the three dimensions of space as being confined to the surface of a balloon. But then what does the radius of the balloon represent, and what does it mean to say that the balloon is being blown up? The answer to this is that the radius of the balloon is a measure of time, and the passage of time has the effect of blowing up the balloon. This will give you a very rough, but useful, idea of the sort of theory investigated by the mathematician.

> The balloon analogy brings out a very important point. It shows we must not imagine that we are situated at the center of the Universe, just because we see all the galaxies to be moving away from us. For, whichever dot you care to choose on the surface of the balloon, you will find that the other dots all move away from it. In other words, whichever galaxy you happen to be in, the other galaxies will appear to be receding from you.[1]

---

[1]Fred Hoyle, *The Nature of the Universe* (New York: Harper & Row Publishers, 1960).

1. What subject is the author explaining?

2. To what is the author comparing his subject?

3. How are these two things alike?

4. Where does the analogy end? That is, how are these two things different?

Life Is Like . . .

Directions: Follow the steps below in writing an analogy comparing "Life" to an object.

1. With a partner, complete the following statements.

   a. Eating an ice cream cone is like

   b. Seeing someone you have missed is like

   c. Having your parent teach you to drive is like

2. Working independently, consider the idea "Life." Brainstorm at least seven reactions to it and write them below. Your reactions might be words, phrases, or sentences.

3. After looking at your reactions, write an analogy that incorporates at least four of them.

Name _____

Date _____

4. Write down the name of an object. Jot down thoughts and associations about that word below.

   Object:_____

   Associations

5. No matter how far-fetched the connections are, list at least four ways this object is similar to "Life."

Life	Object
a.	
b.	
c.	
d.	

6. On a separate piece of paper, write a paragraph explaining your analogy. How is life like_____? Where does the analogy end? Include a drawing or other illustration, if you wish.

Lesson 28
Argumentation and Logic

Objectives

- To become familiar with argumentation

- To recognize inductive and deductive reasoning

- To analyze common fallacies in critical thinking

Notes to the Teacher

The form of persuasion called argument emphasizes the use of sound reasoning to convince the reader that a certain opinion is valid. An argument takes a definite "pro" or "anti" approach to a topic that is open to controversy. In writing this form, the writer commonly uses a calm, rational approach in addressing a reader who is also presumed to be reasonable. Appeals to emotion are subordinated to careful logic.

Most students have a general sense of what is or is not logical, alerting them to discourse that "doesn't make sense." Many may have used principles of induction and deduction in the classroom—particularly in science and math classes. This lesson presents some principles of logic in preparation for students' work on argumentative essays. Their familiarity with argumentation, principles of reasoning, and logical fallacies can be assessed through these activities.

Procedure

1. Ask volunteers to role-play these situations:

   a. A teacher and student talking about a term paper deadline; the students wants an extension, but the teacher wants to hold to the original date.

   b. Two McDonald's employees talking about making more garden salads; one thinks they need more, while the other thinks they have enough.

   c. Two friends talking about the subject of lying; one thinks lying is always wrong, while the other thinks some situations make it both necessary and right.

   After each role play, conduct a brief discussion. Which side was more convincing? Why?

2. Point out that there are times when we want to convince a person to accept an idea—and we are more interested in what the audience thinks than in what it does. Ask students to suggest examples. You may want to stimulate a short brainstorming session with these examples or others: there should/should not be a twelve-month school year; hunting does/does not benefit wildlife; it is/is not good for teenagers to get jobs.

3. Emphasize that in situations where we want to convince someone of an opinion, logical reasoning is essential. Use examples of logic that emerged in the role playing in procedure 1.

4. Have students read part A of **Handout 41**. Take time to answer questions. Then have each student devise examples of induction and deduction. Ask volunteers to share examples with the class.

5. Have students complete part B of the handout.

   Suggested Responses:

   1. *There is insufficient evidence for a conclusion about all high school students.*

   2. *There is accidental, not causal, relationship, between umbrella and weather.*

   3. *Narrow interpretation—green peppers may be stocked daily.*

   4. *Invalid generalization—not everyone likes pepperoni.*

   5. *Each use of the verb "to kill" has a different meaning.*

   6. *Other animals like raw meat, too—Spike could be a cat.*

6. Have students complete part C.

   Suggested Responses:

   a. *Possible student example: I hate all vegetables, but I like carrots and corn.*

   b. *2; The shopper fails to consider other possible causes.*

   c. *4; The generalization about Gene is too hasty; the premise about pepperoni pizza is false.*

d. 2; The businessman mistakes the corre-lation of umbrella/no rain as causation.

e. Possible student examples: Life is like a box of chocolates; don't share what you have or you'll end up with a box of nothing.

f. 5; The use of the word "killing" to mean two different things.

g. 3; The shopper generalizes about the shelf life of peppers with little proof.

h. Possible student example: Candidate B voted for a tax increase forty years ago, so don't re-elect him.

i. Possible student example: Candidate A has no sense of humor and is a terrible dresser, so B would make a better representative.

j. 1; The restaurant manager made a con-clusion about all high school students based on the behavior of a few.

An Introduction to Logic

Part A.

Directions: Read about the processes of induction and deduction. Think about specific instances in which you have used induction and deduction in the past week, and write examples in the spaces provided.

Thinking involves two general kinds or reasoning: induction and deduction.

In induction, we observe specific instances as a basis for forming general conclusions. The experimental method of scientific research exemplifies this thought process, which is also characteristic of everyday life. Examples:

a. The mail truck delivers mail to your new home every day at 11:00 A.M. for two consecutive weeks. You conclude that the daily delivery time is at 11:00 A.M.

b. The mail truck delivers mail to Alfred's new home on Monday at 11:00 A.M., on Tuesday at 3:00 P.M., on Wednesday at noon, and on Thursday not at all. Alfred concludes that the mail delivery schedule is irregular.

In deduction, we use a generalization as a basis for deriving specific conclusions. In studies of logic, deduction is represented by syllogisms. A syllogism consists of a major premise, a minor premise, and a conclusion. Examples:

a. All spiders have eight legs (*major premise*); Charlotte is a spider (*minor premise*); therefore, Charlotte has eight legs (*conclusion*).

b. Team sports are good for young people (*major premise*); football is a team sport (*minor premise*); therefore, football is good for young people (*conclusion*).

Combinations of induction and deduction characterize most of our thinking. Consider how the following experience with the mail truck over a fifteen-day period might affect your logical reasoning:

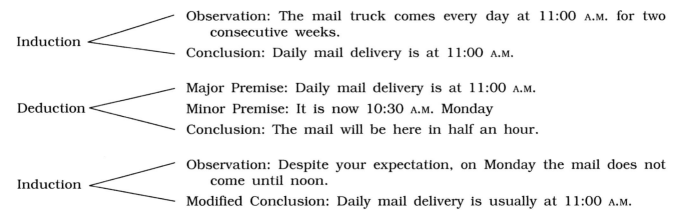

Induction
Observation: The mail truck comes every day at 11:00 A.M. for two consecutive weeks.
Conclusion: Daily mail delivery is at 11:00 A.M.

Deduction
Major Premise: Daily mail delivery is at 11:00 A.M.
Minor Premise: It is now 10:30 A.M. Monday
Conclusion: The mail will be here in half an hour.

Induction
Observation: Despite your expectation, on Monday the mail does not come until noon.
Modified Conclusion: Daily mail delivery is usually at 11:00 A.M.

The process goes on and on as we
- use specifics to formulate general conclusions
- use generalizations to make inferences about other specifics
- use later specifics either to reinforce generalizations or to modify them

Think of something that happens periodically in your own life. Summarize on the chart below how you have used both induction and deduction in drawing conclusions about that event.

Induction
- Observation: _____
  _____
- Conclusion: _____
  _____

Deduction
- Major Premise: _____
  _____
- Minor Premise: _____
  _____
- Conclusion: _____
  _____

Induction
- Observation: _____
  _____
- Modified Conclusion: _____
  _____

Part B.

Directions: Here are some examples of faulty thinking. Use your natural sense of logic to pinpoint the mistakes in reasoning. Briefly explain the faulty reasoning in the space provided.

1. A restaurant manager observes a large group of high school students who come in every afternoon for french fries and sodas. He concludes that all high school students like french fries.

2. A businessman notices that it rains on three consecutive days when he is not carrying an umbrella. He decides to carry an umbrella the next day so that it will not rain.

3. A shopper notices that the green peppers in a store always look fresh and crisp. She concludes that green peppers have a long shelf life.

4. Everyone likes pizza with pepperoni. Gene is a person. Therefore, Gene must like pizza with pepperoni.

5. The proper punishment for killing someone is imprisonment. My score in that chemistry test killed me. Therefore the chemistry teacher should go to jail.

6. All dogs like raw meat. Spike likes raw meat. Therefore, Spike must be a dog.

Part C.

Directions: Read about faulty reasoning below. Then write the number of any statements in part B which each fallacy type appears, and briefly explain the fallacy. (Or, if the fallacy type appears in none of the six examples, offer your own brief example.)

Both induction and deduction demand attention to accuracy and relevance. In induction, false conclusions result when specific observations are insufficient or mistaken. In deduction, invalid conclusions result when premises are inaccurate or their relevance to one another is misinterpreted.

Errors in logical reasoning, sometimes called *fallacies*, can be very difficult to pinpoint. In your own writing and in reading others' works, be alert for these common fallacies:

a. Self-contradiction: statements that cannot be true simultaneously

b. Over-simplification: failing to recognize multiple factors or causes

c. Hasty generalizations: using too little evidence

d. Confusing precedence with causation: mistaking a time relationship for a cause-effect relationship

e. Faulty analogy: extending a comparison beyond reasonable limits

f. Shifts in denotation: using the same word to mean different things

g. Begging the question: making generalizations with no proof

h. Ignoring the question: focusing on irrelevant points or minor issues

i. Appealing to persons instead of issues: a variation of ignoring the question

j. Overly broad generalizations: indiscriminate use of qualifiers like *all* or *none*

Lesson 29
The Essay of Argumentation

Objectives

- To analyze several argumentative essays

- To apply the writing process to essays of argumentation

Notes to the Teacher

We sometimes use the word *argument* to denote an impassioned verbal conflict between two people. In literary terms, however, an argument is a logical presentation of an opinion on a controversial subject. The writer aims to convince the reader of an opinion. Persuasive elements, such as description, figurative language, and emotional appeals, serve only to buttress the force of reasoning.

The materials in this lesson enable students to analyze model arguments before composing original arguments. Their responses to the handouts assess their abilities to analyze and write arguments.

Procedure

1. Write the word *argument* on the board or overhead. Use information from the Notes to the Teacher to define the term.

2. Review some of the key vocabulary in **Handout 42** (*fledgling, colossus, adroit, feinting, hemorrhage, concussion, poleax, prevailing mores*). Then have students complete the handout.

   Suggested Responses:

   1. *the morality of prizefighting*

   2. *against prizefighting*

   3. *interview with an expert; death of a young fighter; investigators' reactions; physiological facts*

   4. *The public's "thirst for blood" is responsible for the continuation of this vicious sport.*

   6. *statistics showing some other sport or activity to be more dangerous; appealing quotes from fighters and trainers; explanation of available safeguards*

   7. *Deductive—Deliberate killing/maiming of human beings is wrong. (assumed)*

   Prizefighting approves killing/maiming human beings.

   8. *The first premise is a generally accepted principle, so the basic syllogism is logical. One sentence seems to reflect the fallacy called "begging the question": "Nature, however, can protect man against everything except man himself" (paragraph 8).*

   If students need extra support in identifying the structure of this essay, share the graphic organizers on the Teacher Resource Page. Encourage students to complete one as they read.

3. Briefly discuss with students what they expect to find in an argument entitled "The Importance of Being a Teenage TV Dropout." Then have students complete **Handout 43**.

   Suggested Responses:

   1. *issue: teenagers' absorption in TV; attitude: negative*

   2. *to dispose of some opposing views*

   3. *humorous and colorful comparison of teens without TV to frogs without lily pads; not overly exploited*

   4. a. *TV absorption prevents interaction with real people.*

      b. *It causes a passive lifestyle.*

      c. *It inhibits creativity.*

      d. *It stifles conversational skills.*

   5. *Deduction: Growth in vitality is necessary for teenage health. Television saps vitality. Therefore, television is destructive to teens. This conclusion is then related to an unsupported generalization (Whatever is harmful to teens should be banned from their lives.) to lead to the author's conclusion.*

   7. *clear and logical explanation of some negative results of TV absorption*

   Encourage students to discuss reactions to the essay. You may want to point out that the essay is partly satiric, and that the unsupported generalization would offer an opening for refuting the argument.

173

4. Have small groups complete the first steps of **Handout 44**. If necessary, review how to come up with a focused thesis statement (Lesson 18).

5. Direct students to use the rest of the handout as a guide in the process of writing essays of argumentation. Have them review the handout, and allow an opportunity for clarifying questions

6. **Handout 45** contains a rubric to use in guiding and assessing the final draft. Students should have a copy of this evaluation guide on hand while writing.

7. Establish a reasonable deadline for completing the essay. A week to ten days should be sufficient.

Graphic Organizers

Cause-and-Effect Map

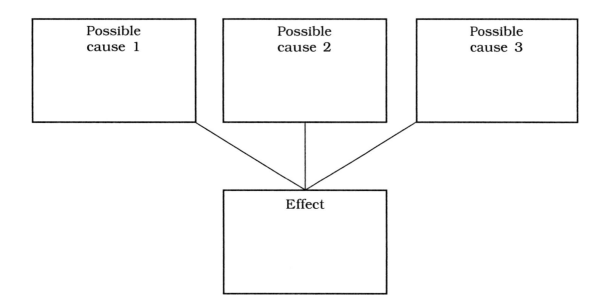

Spider Map

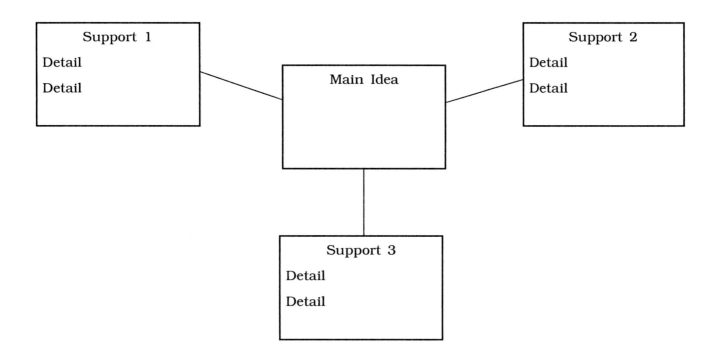

Reading for Argument

Directions: Below is an essay about a prizefighter who was killed in the ring. Before you read the essay, look at the questions that follow it. As you read, ask yourself what argument Norman Cousins is making. How does he structure his writing to convince you to share his opinion? Mark any words or phrases that help you follow his train of thought more easily or that are especially persuasive. When you have finished reading the essay, answer the questions and be prepared to discuss your answers.

Who Killed Benny Paret?

Sometime about 1935 or 1936 I had an interview with Mike Jacobs, the prize-fight promoter. I was a fledgling newspaper reporter at that time; my beat was education, but during the vacation season I found myself on varied assignments, all the way from ship news to sports reporting. In this way I found myself sitting opposite the most powerful figure in the boxing world.

There was nothing spectacular in Mr. Jacobs's manner or appearance; but when he spoke about prize fights, he was no longer a bland little man but a colossus who sounded the way Napoleon must have sounded when he reviewed a battle. You knew you were listening to Number One. His saying something made it true.

We discussed what to him was the only important element in successful promoting—how to please the crowd. So far as he was concerned, there was no mystery to it. You put killers in the ring and the people filled your arena. You hire boxing artists—men who are adroit at feinting, parrying, weaving, jabbing, and dancing, but who don't pack dynamite in their fists—and you wind up counting your empty seats. So you searched for the killers and sluggers and maulers—fellows who could hit with the force of a baseball bat.

I asked Mr. Jacobs if he was speaking literally when he said people came out to see the killer.

"They don't come out to see a tea party," he said evenly. "They come out to see the knockout. They come out to see a man hurt. If they think anything else, they're kidding themselves."

Recently a young man by the name of Benny Paret was killed in the ring. The killing was seen by millions; it was on television. In the twelfth round he was hit hard in the head several times, went down, was counted out, and never came out of the coma.

The Paret fight produced a flurry of investigations. Governor Rockefeller was shocked by what happened and appointed a committee to assess the responsibility. The New York State Boxing Commission decided to find out what was wrong. The District Attorney's office expressed its concern. One question that was solemnly studied in all three probes concerned the action of the referee. Did he act in time to stop the fight? Another question had to do with the role of the examining doctors who certified the physical fitness of the fighters before the bout. Still another question involved Mr. Paret's manager; did he rush his boy into the fight without adequate time to recuperate from the previous one?

In short, the investigators looked into every possible cause except the real one. Benny Paret was killed because the human fist delivers enough impact, when directed against the head, to produce a massive hemorrhage in the brain. The human brain is the most delicate and complex mechanism in all creation. It has a lacework of millions of highly fragile nerve connections. Nature attempts to protect this exquisitely intricate machinery by encasing it in a hard shell. Fortunately, the shell is thick enough to withstand a great deal of pounding. Nature, however, can protect man against everything except man himself. Not every blow to the head will kill a man—but there is always the risk of concussion and damage to the brain. A prize fighter may be able to survive even repeated brain concussions and go on fighting, but the damage to his brain may be permanent.

In any event, it is futile to investigate the referee's role and seek to determine whether he should have intervened to stop the fight earlier. This is not where the primary responsibility lies. The primary responsibility lies with the people who pay to see a man hurt. The referee who stops a fight too soon from the crowd's viewpoint can expect to be booed. The crowd wants the knockout; it wants to see a man stretched out on the canvas. This is the supreme moment in boxing. It is nonsense to talk about prize fighting as a test of boxing skills. No crowd was ever brought to its feet screaming and cheering at the sight of two men beautifully dodging and weaving out of each other's jabs. The time the crowd comes alive is when a man is hit hard over the heart or the head, when his mouthpiece flies out, when blood squirts out of his nose or eyes, when he wobbles under the attack and his pursuer continues to smash at him with poleax impact.

Don't blame it on the referee. Don't even blame it on the fight managers. Put the blame where it belongs—on the prevailing mores that regard prize fighting as a perfectly proper enterprise and vehicle of entertainment. No one doubts that many people enjoy prize fighting and will miss it if it should be thrown out. And that is precisely the point.[1]

1. Identify the central issue in this argument.

2. What is Cousins's position on this issue?

3. What evidence supports his position?

4. Identify the main point in the concluding paragraph.

5. Does this essay succeed in convincing you to share Cousins's opinion? Why or why not?

6. If you were going to write an argument refuting this one, what approaches might you use?

7. Is "Who Killed Benny Paret?" basically inductive or deductive? Explain.

8. Evaluate the overall logic of Cousins's article. Do you note any fallacies or weaknesses in his reasoning?

[1]Norman Cousins, "Who Killed Benny Paret?" *Present Tense: An American Editor's Odyssey* (New York: McGraw-Hill, 1967).

A Sample Argument

Directions: The following essay about TV-watching was written by a teacher as a sample argument. As you read the essay carefully, try to hear the speaker's tone of voice. Notice how the writer uses analogies, comparison/contrast, and inductive/deductive reasoning to make her point, and mark any particularly effective supports. Finally, answer the questions that follow the essay and be prepared to discuss your responses.

The Importance of Being a Teenage TV Dropout

In homes across the nation, teens lie comfortably on their unmade beds before a TV set perched on a stand. It is evident from the position of their eyes and the tilt of their heads that they are mesmerized by the moving colors and variegated sounds emerging from that hallowed device. If you are not lucky enough to have a personal TV, no matter. Teens can spread out on shag rugs specially designed for TV viewing in dens, rec rooms, and basements. Since these electronic gadgets have sapped the vitality of adolescents for over thirty years, TV should be outlawed from homes where teenagers live.

TV certainly has its merits. Certain segments of the population cannot and should not be deprived of hours of TV's varied programming. Latchkey children are among those most in need of its benefits. When they come home from school, the flick of a dial can provide companions to entertain them until Mom or Dad arrive home from work. Preschool children have two great needs TV can fulfill. The first is the need to learn letters and numbers before they meet these complex concepts in a place called school. The second need is even greater than the first. TV can be a benevolent babysitter while Mother cooks, cleans, and does the laundry. It can keep them from wandering about the house or yard, starting fires, cutting themselves with knives or terrorizing the neighbors. The third segment of society that needs the services of TV includes senior citizens, who must while away the hours that may sometimes weigh heavily on their hands.

Assuredly there will be critics who oppose the soundness of the arguments presented here. Some critics will maintain that teens without TVs are like frogs without a pad in a lily pond. They would have no place from which to look placidly upon the world as it moves rapidly by. With bulging eyes staring straight ahead, the frog occasionally snaps up a flying insect. Teens, too, have their eyes glued to one spot, but when an uninteresting commercial appears, they dash into the kitchen for an assortment of junk food. Other critics, who believe teens should sally forth once in a while, say TV teaches them what to wear, what to eat and drink, where to go for entertainment, and what hot new items they can purchase to make them like everyone else. The more intellectual critics feel that TV is an indispensable learning tool. It pours astounding amounts of facts into teenage brains, clear images of the national and world situations and vast stores of trivia that cannot be found in any encyclopedia or textbook.

But there are a number of dangers that critics and teens must consider before objecting to the removal of TV sets. First, watching TV for hours on end prevents teens from meeting real people. Of course, one does see real people on news broadcasts, talk shows, and documentaries. TV, however, is not conducive to exchanging a handshake, a smile or a comment. It is, therefore, better to encounter real people in supermarkets where one goes to do the family shopping. Real people are also found in hospitals, in homes for the mentally retarded, and in nearby residences for senior citizens. These real people need a smile, a song performed by a choral group from school, or a performance by a clown troupe. The blind and the elderly, who are also real people, might need someone to go shopping for them, or write a letter or read a favorite passage from the Bible. The resulting feeling of joy and satisfaction cannot be had from watching a sitcom or a crime drama.

TV viewing also has an adverse effect on a teen's ability to participate actively in life. Watching the football hero make the winning touchdown is one thing; making the TD yourself is entirely different. Seeing and hearing the Boston Pops on TV playing a rousing Sousa march might prove inspiring, but getting out on the field at half time with a trumpet in hand is a far more spirited experience. Seeing the TV detective solve the mystery and get the girl is memorable for a moment, but hearing the audience applaud at the school play lasts a lifetime. Being active and passive are poles apart, as any English student knows. Reclining passively before a TV set, the teen may view other young people protesting human rights violations or USA involvement in Central America. The active approach involves reaching out to a teen who is left out of the crowd or writing the mayor asking him for low-cost homes for the poor.

Watching TV also inhibits the use of a teen's imagination and creativity. How often have English students heard their teachers say, "Use your creativity and ingenuity in writing this essay"? The effect on teens of this imperative is more often than not a tightening of the throat muscles and a sinking feeling in the pit of the stomach. If there were no TVs in homes, students' minds would be crammed with images from poetry, from nature, from life in the city. To write a descriptive essay, all students would have to do is conjure up in their mind's eye a few of Frost's rural images and add them to their own: the swans on the lake in the park, cows grazing in the meadow, the pond in the woods behind Grandpa's house.

To write a persuasive essay the recipe is the same: to Sandburg's city images add the pictures of a modern city, the homeless women tightly clutching their possessions, men sleeping over sidewalk grates, and children with eyes filled with hopelessness standing in line with their parents, a line that stretches for blocks, waiting for the soup kitchen to open its doors. Writing passionately of the structures that create such misery and offering solutions and measures to be taken to eliminate it would complete the assignment, all without the aid of TV.

TV viewing also prevents teens from becoming socialized and lessens their power of carrying on a conversation with people of every age and occupation. One person who is taken for granted in most households is Mother, with whom many teens hold only limited communication, usually by means of single sentences or simply a nod in response to questions. If Mother inquires if the day at school was profitable or if they have cleaned their rooms, they give a nod and immediately turn their attention to other matters. When dashing through the kitchen minutes before the supper hour, teenage boys often hurl in her direction, "What's for supper, Ma?" Of course they seldom wait for a reply. It rarely occurs to some that Mother is an intelligent, literate human with opinions on current events and expertise in a variety of fields. Having read in *Consumer Reports* the nutritional value of cereals like Shredded Wheat, Fiber One, and Sugar Smacks, she could share some information that would be of value when preparing a report for a class in Family Living or economics. Dad, too, might appreciate hearing a few coherent sentences instead of the perennial, "Aw, gee, do I hafta?" when he asks for help in cleaning the garage or trimming the hedges. Asking him which bait is better for catching walleye, artificial lures or suckers, might result in a rather lengthy discussion held not in the garage but possibly on the way to the stream or lake. Little sister also needs

179

a word from big brother now and then. Inquiring how many baseball cards she has already collected may result in a puzzled stare the first time, but a satisfying sharing after she gets used to the idea that the interest shown in her collection is genuine. Actually having an intelligent conversation with family members and others of the human race might just prove to be a suitable substitute for the one-sided monologue delivered by the TV set.

Television—who needs it? Not the healthy, intelligent, witty American adolescent. Although TV may be informative and entertaining, it is a spectator sport and no substitute for real living. Becoming a social being and a fine conversationalist, able to talk with adults, peers and little children with equal facility, is more advantageous than being able to rattle off the names of the stars of sit-coms. Showing compassion to the needy is more fulfilling than watching the statistics on the homeless and the hungry rise daily. Using talents that have gone undeveloped for years brings delight not only to the individual, but also to parents and others who are beneficiaries of their endeavors. Fear not. The TV industry will not go bankrupt if television sets are removed from the homes of teens. The nation will improve significantly. The enemies of the United States will wonder at the vitality and vibrancy of its citizens and future leaders. They will no longer hurl insults and criticism at its citizens, for they will no longer behold vacant staring eyes and heedless ears, but psyches attuned to the needs of all humanity.

1. Identify the central issue and author's point of view.

2. What is the purpose of the second paragraph?

3. Analyze the analogy in the third paragraph. What is being compared? How are these two things alike? Is this a good analogy?

4. List the reasons the author cites to support this argument's position.

5. Is this argument primarily inductive or deductive? Explain.

6. Do you find it convincing? Why or why not?

7. Evaluate the essay's overall logic. Do you note any fallacies or weaknesses?

8. If this were a preliminary draft and you were conferencing with the author about it, what suggestions would you make?

Name _____

Date _____

Writing an Argument

Directions: Complete the following steps to prepare your essay of argumentation. Submit this handout with your final draft.

1. Finding a Good Topic

   Half the battle in argumentation is settling on a topic about which you have genuine, strong opinions. The subject may be as universal as truth or beauty, as public as capital punishment or cigarette smoking in restaurants, or as personal as having a pet hamster or being an only child. Brainstorm possible issues and record them here.

2. Making a Preliminary Statement

   Select an issue, think about it, and write a sentence expressing your starting position.

3. Target Audience

   To whom will you address your argument?

4. Pinpointing Pros and Cons

   Read about your topic; talk to other people who know about it. Think about not only pros (reasons for holding your opinion), but cons (opposing reasons that you will need to rebut).

Pros	Cons

5. Writing a Thesis

   State your topic and position in one clear sentence.

6. Organizing Your Content

   Identify the main factors in the opposing view (see your list of "cons") and suggest ways to dispose of them.

   Identify the main factors supporting your view (see your list of "pros") and suggest evidence, examples, and analogies.

7. Writing Rough Drafts

   Choose one of these two organizational schemes and draft your essay of argumentation.

   a. Introduction, state thesis
      Most important reason
      Second important reason
      Third important reason
      Rebut opposing argument 1
      Rebut opposing argument 2
      Rebut opposing argument 3
      Conclusion

   b. Introduction, state thesis
      Reason 1
      Opposing argument 1
      Reason 2
      Opposing argument 2
      Reason 3
      Opposing argument 3
      Conclusion

8. Conferencing Yourself

   Read the rough draft aloud to yourself and review it for logic, clarity, organization, and effective wording. Does your essay say what you mean? Is it convincing? Are the connections clear? Do you like it? Then write a revised draft.

9. Consulting Reader-Reactors

    Ask two or three readers to respond to your paper. In the space below, record their responses to questions like these:

    a. What do you think my main point is?

    b. Have I convinced you? Why or why not?

    c. Did you enjoy my essay? Why or why not?

    d. Do you have any suggestions?

Reader 1	Reader 2
a.	a.
b.	b.
c.	c.
d.	d.

10. Finalizing the Argument

    After considering your readers' responses, write your final draft. Refer to **Handout 45,** the evaluation rubric, as you write.

11. Completing the Assignment

    Assemble your final paper with the previous drafts, this handout, and **Handout 45**. Be sure to label each draft clearly by number and date.

Name _____

Date _____

Argumentative Essay Evaluation

Directions: Each of the following criteria will be given a score. Use this rubric as a guide while completing your assignment.

Criteria	Points	
1. The writer uses persuasive techniques.	_____	/8
2. The style and content are suited to the target audience.	_____	/8
3. The essay expresses and fulfills a purpose.	_____	/8
4. The main idea is clearly stated.	_____	/8
5. Supporting ideas are included.	_____	/8
6. The writer demonstrates a knowledge of subject.	_____	/8
7. Each paragraph has a main idea.	_____	/8
8. All paragraphs are relevant.	_____	/8
9. All paragraphs are well-organized.	_____	/8
10. The writer uses analogies.	_____	/8
11. The writer uses inductive/deductive logic.	_____	/8
12. The mechanics are correct.	_____	/4
13. There is sentence variety.	_____	/4
14. Action verbs are used.	_____	/4
15. Colorful, detailed language is used.	_____	/4
16. The writer demonstrates word economy.	_____	/4
17. Transitions are smooth.	_____	/4
Total Points	_____	/112

Lesson 30
Economy and Elaboration

Objective
- To edit with particular attention to economy and elaboration

Notes to the Teacher

Why are revision and editing necessary? This is a question you have probably heard from your students. Why isn't the personal outpouring of thoughts in a first draft sufficient? If students' ownership is paramount, shouldn't they decide at what point the paper expresses their ideas? After revision and editing, some students might feel that their paper has become unfamiliar, no longer their own—an artificial composition that satisfies the teacher and the standards of formal English, but not their own hearts. Anticipating revision and editing might even clog their first draft creativity and reinforce insecurity about their writing: "What's the use? I'm still going to get a lousy grade." Even worse, an emphasis on editing might teach students how to write but result in their not liking to write (an attitude shared by many adults).

What's the alternative? An anything-goes, every-essay-is-sterling approach? Obviously, that too would be disastrous. Writing teachers are therefore caught in a delicate balancing act: encouraging students in their current writing, while guiding them to improved writing. Revising and editing are part of that direction, part of that human paradox of actuality and potentiality—we are fine as we are, but we can do better and be better. Students will have the opportunity to become better, editing their own sentences in the exercises, and providing examples for teacher assessment and guidance.

Here are three reasons for revising and editing.

1. Communication

Except for private writing, students write to a public—in this case, an English-speaking public with specific criteria for reading comprehension. Writing ownership, like personal freedom, is never absolute, but shaped and compromised by the needs of society.

We write grammatically to help our readers to understand.

2. Challenge

Part of learning and enjoying any skill is the anticipation of improvement. The feeling of overcoming obstacles builds self-esteem. Most students, despite their balking, do enjoy the challenge of transforming murky writing to clean writing. The challenge for teachers is knowing the right difficulty level for each student, which can raise from correcting run-ons to composing sophisticated structures.

3. Creativity

Creativity, for most people, does not involve inventing brand new patterns, but discovering alternate ones. The English language has numerous stylistic patterns: a love letter, a research paper, a note to the babysitter, instructions for assembling a bicycle, free verse poetry, a sonnet, stream-of-consciousness fiction, and factual newspaper stories, to name a few. The more patterns students learn and master, the more resources they will have for creative expression.

Procedure

1. Stimulate a discussion about revision/rewriting by asking, "How do you feel about rewriting your work? What don't you like about it? What do you like? Why are students asked to rewrite? Why do professional writers often go through several drafts? In what ways are the later versions often improvements over the earlier ones?"

2. Distribute **Handout 46** and instruct students to complete part A. Explain that it outlines three reasons for rewriting and requires them to rate how they feel about the six activities of the writing process.

3. After students have completed the handout, allow them to discuss their ratings.

Conduct a class discussion of their feelings and attitudes toward writing. Students may simply enjoy airing their views and receiving teacher empathy.

4. Review what students learned about word economy (*the idea that in writing, less is often better*) in Lesson 20. Ask students one technique they learned for achieving word economy. Students may be interested to learn that in 1998 President Clinton signed a memorandum requiring federal agencies to write customers in plain language. Now there are even "Plain Language" awards for government writers who submit exemplary improvements to unclear federal correspondence. (See the Plain Language Action Network's Web site at http://www.plainlanguage.gov.)

5. Explain that part B of the handout offers five other ways to economize wording and go over that part of the handout with students. These techniques require a level of writing sophistication some of your students may not have, so you may choose to focus simply on "removing unnecessary and repeated words." However, most students enjoy "reducing" sentences. (See *Writing 1*, Lesson 18, or any good composition handbook for additional practice.) The exercise requires students to select two sentences from their own essay for reduction; more could be required.

6. Introduce the idea of elaboration—expanding an idea to include greater detail. Point out that economy and elaboration are both goals of good writing; one does not preclude the other. A good piece of writing contains no unneeded words (*economy*), but it also contains enough supportive detail (*elaboration*).

7. Direct students to complete part C of the handout. This section on elaboration presumes even more student sophistication than the previous one on economy, so use your discretion in assigning it. Consider first giving students a few sample sentences to expand. (See *Writing 1*, Lesson 18).

Revising a Composition

Part A.

Directions: Maybe you have asked yourself, "Why isn't my first draft good enough? Why do I have to revise and edit?" Read the reasons for revision below. Then rate your preferences for each of the six steps in the writing process.

1. Communication

   Except for journals and private notes, your writing is directed at an audience. To understand and appreciate your ideas, that audience—in this case, an English-speaking one—presupposes that certain rules and patterns are followed. The more closely you revise and edit, the more clearly you communicate your ideas to that audience.

2. Challenge

   If you just started playing piano and expected to be a classical pianist in six months, you would probably get frustrated and quit. However, if you expected to learn the scales and a simple song, you would be more likely to enjoy your practice. Most of us like challenges when we have a good chance of success. The same is true in writing. The challenges of revising and editing are hurdles, opportunities for growth—not stumbling blocks.

3. Creativity

   Would you wear a bathing suit to a wedding? Or a thick overcoat to a warm picnic? Just as different settings call for different dress, varied purposes and audiences call for varied writing styles. Creative writers, like creative dressers, learn many styles. Sometimes a poem expresses their ideas best, other times an essay. By learning formal English, you are learning another way to express yourself.

Take a few minutes to think about how you usually feel about each of these six steps in the writing process. How do you like these various activities? Circle a number for each 1 = not at all; 10 = very much.

Prewriting   1 2 3 4 5 6 7 8 9 10

Drafting   1 2 3 4 5 6 7 8 9 10

Conferencing   1 2 3 4 5 6 7 8 9 10

Revising   1 2 3 4 5 6 7 8 9 10

Editing   1 2 3 4 5 6 7 8 9 10

Publishing   1 2 3 4 5 6 7 8 9 10

Part B.

Directions: Read about ways to achieve word economy below, and complete the exercise.

Have you ever asked someone a question and received a ten-minute answer when a two-minute response would have sufficed? None of us likes to waste time hearing needless information. In writing, getting to the point is called *word economy*. If you can express the same idea in seven pages or five, three paragraphs or two, twelve words or eight, choose the shorter. The reader will appreciate it.

Ways to achieve word economy:

1. Use the active voice.

    The trees were shaken by the wind.
    The wind shook the trees.

2. Reduce clauses to prepositional phrases.

    The man who is wearing the green hat is my uncle.
    The man with the green hat is my uncle.

3. Reduce clauses and phrases to single words.

    I want a dog that has spots.
    I want a spotted dog.

4. Reduce clauses to appositives.

    Mr. Winters, who is a carpenter, is building our back porch.
    Mr. Winters, a carpenter, is building our back porch.

5. Reduce clauses to participle, gerund, or infinitive phrases.

    He found his wallet when he decided to look under the chair.
    Looking under the chair, he found his wallet.

6. Get to the point.

    Abraham Lincoln, without a doubt, although my brother, who always disagrees with me, might take exception just to irritate me, was a fine president.
    Abraham Lincoln was a fine president, whatever my brother might say.

Select two sentences in your essay and rewrite them, reducing the number of words. Place the before-and-after versions here:

1. a.

    b.

2. a.

    b.

Part C.

Directions: Read about ways to accomplish elaboration, and complete the exercise.

Elaboration—expanding an idea with examples, reasons, and descriptive details—is not a contradiction of economy. To achieve economy, a writer eliminates needless words. To accomplish elaboration, the writer adds words that supply new ideas. Elaboration often involves providing more detail about who, what, when, where, why, and how.

1. Elaborate on your general descriptive statements with particulars and details.

   Supplying precise details about how something looks, sounds, feels, tastes, and smells like often helps the reader better comprehend what you are trying to communicate.

   She has unusual eyes.

   Her deeply set emerald eyes peer out through long, black eyelashes.

2. Illustrate general statements with instances and examples.

   To ease a pet's grief over the loss of a person, plan ahead.

   If family members know that someone important to the pet is leaving the home, other family members should start spending more time with the pet before the departure.

3. Offer reasons for an opinion or statement.

   That is a really good movie.

   That movie pulls you in, challenges your prejudices, shakes your world, and leaves you laughing.

4. Provide definitions of particular words whose meanings may not be clear to your reader.

   Penelope is an ecologist.

   Penelope is an ecologist, a scientist who studies the relationships between plants, animals, and the environment around them.

5. When describing an object or process, provide details about logical divisions or steps.

   That rock tumbler kit makes polishing stones a long and boring process.

   The rock tumbler kit takes too long to prepare and does too much for you. You mix the water and powders, set up the machine, and wait around for three weeks while it tumbles the rocks in the solution.

Select two sentences from your essay and rewrite them, becoming more specific through elaborating details. The new version may be longer than one sentence.

1. a.

   b.

2. a.

   b.

Part 7
Responding to Literature

Most English students—especially those in college prep classes—are asked at some point to write an essay response to a literary work. Many students enjoy reading book, movie, and music reviews and write reviews for school newspapers. But the transfer of the writing process from general writing to the specific form of literary response/analysis does not always come easily.

This section focuses on poetry. Prewriting exercises encourage the reader to interact with the poems; understanding and appreciation are prerequisites for effective critical writing. Each lesson builds toward a composition experience and directs students to follow the six-activity writing process. Be sure to allow sufficient drafting and revision time.

The handouts include the poems used for response and analysis. Incorporating additional selections from the class's literature text, or from a collection of Young Adult poetry, may be helpful.

Lesson 31
Poetry Analysis: First Steps

Objectives
- To understand that analysis is a universal, adaptable skill
- To analyze poetry

Notes to the Teacher
The Greeks had the word for it: the poet is a maker, a craftsman who designs ideas with words, just as the sculptor shapes an image in marble or bronze. Aristotle's four causes can be introduced here: The material cause is the idea, the word that will embody it. The formal cause is the pattern or shape the poet will give the idea. The efficient cause is the poet, and the final cause, the reason for writing the poem, may be the strong feeling the writer has about the subject or the need to celebrate an event. As Robert Frost said, "A complete poem is one where emotion has found its thought and the thought has found the words."

Many young people like to take toys, clocks, or radios apart to find out how they work. Some teens like to take cars or computers apart, examine the parts, and replace or improve them. In doing so, they are using analysis (taking apart) and its partner, synthesis (putting together). In biology, students dissect worms, frogs, and cats to see how the organs are placed and to compare them with the human arrangement. In chemistry, they break down unknown solutions to find the components. In history, they divide the long story of human life into manageable periods and then try to see each part in relation to the whole picture.

In analyzing poetry, first we look at the whole, then examine the parts. We want to find out how the poet communicated his or her message through the arrangement of ideas, words, and emotions in a pleasing pattern. Analysis is not a surgical process. It is more like examining a rose, remembering that it was once only a seed, which took root in good soil; grew a stem, leaves, pistil, sepal, and petals; and remained wrapped tightly until sun and moisture opened the bud to the thing of beauty it is. This lesson is an exercise in prewriting analysis—in looking at the parts of a poem and how they work together before writing about one's response to the poem as a whole. Sample poems allow students to practice this skill, and you to assess the necessary pace of future lessons.

If the poems reprinted in this lesson are inappropriate for your students, consider using poems from one of the following Young Adult collections.

- *American Sports Poems*, R. R. Knudson and May Swenson
- *Neighborhood Odes*, Gary Soto
- *Gary Soto: New and Selected Poems*
- *Ordinary Things: Poems from a Walk in Early Spring*, Ralph Fletcher, et. al.
- *This Same Sky: A Collection of Poems from Around the World*, Naomi Shihab Nye, ed.
- *Wherever Home Begins: 100 Contemporary Poems*, Paul Janeczko

For example, instead of having students analyze the sonnet by Shakespeare, you could have them read the more modern "Sonnet XVII" by Ted Berrigan in *Selected Poems: Ted Berrigan*, ed. Aram Saroyan (New York: Penguin Books, 1994) and analyze Berrigan's use of alliteration, imagery, rhyme, etc.

Procedure
1. Write this short poem by Emily Dickinson on the board or on a transparency for the overhead projector. Have a student read it aloud.

   There is no Frigate like a Book
   To take us Lands away
   Nor any Coursers like a Page
   of prancing Poetry—
   This Traverse may the poorest take
   Without oppress of Toll—
   How frugal is the Chariot
   That bears the Human soul.

2. Then ask:

   a. What do you see as you listen to this poem? Explain the first four lines. (*A book may take us very quickly to far-away places and so can a page of poetry. Frigate is a fast warship; coursers, a word for horses that conjures up an image of Arabian horses or any thoroughbred. Poetry, like the thoroughbred, prances rather than plods and can carry the mind swiftly on a far journey.*)

   b. Can you name some books that have taken you "lands away"? Can you think of at least one poem that has really had an impact on you?

3. Explain that this lesson is designed to help students analyze poetry like Dickinson's so that they can understand it and ultimately write a response to it, which is something they are often required to do. Share general information about analysis from Notes to the Teacher. Discuss key literary analysis terms used in this lesson: *stanza, complete/imperfect rhyme, rhyme scheme, metric feet, iambic pentameter, measure, ballad stanza, alliteration, Italian and English sonnet form, couplet, quatrain, image, allusion.* These are contained in the glossary of most literary anthologies.

4. Return to the poem at hand. Ask:

   a. What words in the last four lines are used in an unusual way? (*Traverse and* oppress *are verbs, here used as nouns. The usual subject-verb-object order is sometimes reversed. For instance, the speaker says, "How frugal is the chariot" instead of "The chariot is frugal."*)

   b. Where does the speaker make statements contradictory to what we might expect? (*We don't expect the poorest to be able to take a trip without paying any toll. We don't expect a chariot—a noble kind of vehicle—to be "frugal.")* What point is she making by these seeming contradictions? (*Books and poetry are not—like so many other things—only for those with money; they are inexpensive ways to carry a person beyond normal physical confines.*)

   c. As you listen to the poem and read it aloud, what do you notice about the sounds and rhythms? (*It has a lilting, regular rhythm; alliteration—repeated initial consonants—"prancing poetry".*)

   Explain that Emily Dickinson's model was drawn from the hymn books of the mid- to late 1800s. The pattern Dickinson used resembles a simple ballad pattern. A ballad stanza is a four-line stanza rhyming in the second and fourth lines, having four metrical feet in the first and third lines, and three in the second and fourth. Nevertheless, she never let a mechanical device hinder her original expression of a thought. For example, "away" and "poetry" are near-rhymes, also known as imperfect rhymes; she did not force exact rhymes into these slots.

5. Ask each person to write one question about the poem that has not yet been answered. The question may concern meaning, word usage, or imagery. Allow time for answering the questions. Encourage students to answer each other.

6. Review the Italian and English sonnet forms. Have a student put the two rhyme schemes on the board (*Italian: abba/abba/cde/cde; English: abab/cded/efef/gg*). Remind them of the division of the subject. The Italian sonnet usually poses a question or problem in the first eight lines, an answer or solution in the last six. English sonnets also use this division, but Shakespeare usually takes the first twelve for the problem and the last two for the solution.

7. Remind students that this fourteen-line, patterned poem has been a challenge to many poets. Another element of the pattern is the iambic pentameter rhythm, one unaccented syllable and one accented syllable in each measure, and five measures, or feet, to a line. Originally, in Italy, the sonnets were love songs written by the lover for his lady. When the pattern became popular in England, the subject was extended beyond love songs to include friendship, nature, religion, and death.

8. Distribute **Handout 47**. Have the class read the sonnet silently, then have a volunteer read it aloud. Ask:

   a. What main point is the poet making about life? (*Remaining span of life is very short, so he wishes his friend would appreciate it while he is still with him.*)

   b. To what three things does the poet compare this shortness of life? (*late autumn—season; twilight of one day—a very short time; last few minutes of a fire dying on a hearth*)

   c. Each quatrain (four lines) is one sentence. What three images of autumn does the poet see reflected in himself? (*Few yellow leaves remain on the trees; the boughs shake in the cold; bare boughs are like empty choirs because the birds who sang on them have left. Some readers see an allusion to the ruins of the monks' churches where they had once gathered to sing praise to God.*)

   d. Consider the images in the second quatrain. In what images of the passing day does the poet see himself reflected? (*Twilight—shortest time of the day after sunset before darkness takes over; black night takes even this trace of day away; night, death's counterpart, seals all in sleep.*)

   e. In the third quatrain, what images do you find? (*glowing of fire—just embers—no longer a leaping flame; ashes of his youth—what is left of log rests in ashes; the fire has consumed the wood, so—with nothing left to feed on—it goes out*)

   f. How does the poet draw all his images together in the last two lines? (*He states the following: Now that the friend realizes the poet will not be around too much longer, the friend's love for him will grow stronger. Humans usually cling tightly to some thing or person that they are about to lose.*)

9. Tell students that they have just traced the thought structure of the sonnet. Now have them apply the elements of the sound structures which they reviewed at the beginning of the lesson. Let them mark the rhyming pattern and the metric pattern on their handouts and underscore the alliteration (*cold . . . choirs, sweet . . . sang, seest . . . such . . . sunset, by and by black . . . , second self . . . seals*).

10. Ask students to complete **Handout 47, part B**, by writing a personal response to this poem.

11. Divide the class into groups of four to share their responses to the sonnet. Have students stay in the same group for this entire poetry sequence. Circulate among the groups to answer any questions students may have. You may wish to share your own response with them.

12. Distribute **Handout 48**. Explain that the class will be reading poems by Robert Herrick (1591–1674), Rita Dove (1952–), Edna St. Vincent Millay (1892–1950), and Robert Frost (1875–1963). Before students read the Herrick poems, supply some background information. Tell them the legend of the Hesperides—three maidens (nymphs) who guarded the golden apples of Juno (queen of the gods) in a garden in the west. Point out that Herrick entitled the book in which the two poems reprinted on the handouts are found *Hesperides*. Some think that he was hinting that his poems are precious "golden apples" of Devonshire in southwestern England. Since Hesperus is the evening star, the poems also may be little stars. Herrick loved the Roman poet Horace, whose philosophy of carpe diem, "seize the day," seemed to fit his own philosophy of life.

13. After students have read the poems, ask:

   a. Where does your mind go as you read each poem?

   b. What do the poems have in common? (*themes—shortness of life, enjoy it while you can*)

   c. How are they different? (*Responses will vary. Some students may note that the first is are seventeenth century; the next four are modern American.*)

   d. To whom is each poem addressed? (*Millay to her love; Herrick, to daffodils; Frost, to a friend and to a general reader; Dove, to a general reader*)

Have each group select any two of these poems for comparison with Sonnet 73.

14. Have groups compose their own questions to help them discover how each poem is structured in sound and meaning. Point out that only the Millay poem is a sonnet; the others have varying sound patterns. Frost uses rhyming couplets, while Herrick uses a kind of ballad pattern like Emily Dickinson's. Dove does not use a formal rhyme scheme, but there are many subtle rhymes: *memorial* and *grill*, *galloped* and *dollop*.

15. After each group has prepared all of its questions, direct each person to write a comparison of one poem to Sonnet 73. The completion of the next five activities of the writing process, including conferencing, is left as the students' responsibility. Set a reasonable date for papers to be submitted—two or three days, perhaps.

Name _____

Date _____

Sonnet 73

Part A.

Directions: Read the following poem in which the speaker reflects on getting old. As you read, consider what the speaker is saying to his friend about their relationship—and why. Be prepared for class discussion.

> That time of year thou mayst in me behold
> When yellow leaves, or none, or few, do hang
> Upon those boughs which shake against the cold,
> Bare ruin'd choirs, where late the sweet birds sang.
> In me thou see'st the twilight of such day
> As after sunset fadeth in the west,
> Which by and by black night doth take away,
> Death's second self, that seals up all in rest.
> In me thou see'st the glowing of such fire,
> That on the ashes of his youth doth lie
> As the deathbed whereon it must expire,
> Consumed with that which it was nourished by.
>> This thou perceivest, which makes thy love more strong,
>> To love that well which thou must leave ere long.

—William Shakespeare

Part B.

Directions: Write a personal response to the poem. You might consider these questions:

- Is the speaker's message relevant to my life?
- Does this poem remind me of anything I have ever thought or experienced or read about?
- Have I ever found myself attached to something I would have to leave soon?
- If I were to update this poem, what three images would I use?

Name _____

Date _____

Poems to Analyze

Part A.

Directions: Read these poems twice. The first time, concentrate on each speaker's voice and seeing what he or she describes. The second time, think about how these poems are alike—and how they differ. Jot down any reactions, questions, or comments in the margins.

To Daffodils

Fair daffodils, we weep to see
    You haste away so soon:
As yet the early-rising sun
    Has not attained his noon.
      Stay, stay,
    Until the hasting day
      Has run
    But to the evensong;
And, having pray'd together, we
    Will go with you along.
We have short time to stay, as you;
    We have as short a spring;
As quick a growth to meet decay,
    As you or anything.
      We die,
As your hours do, and dry
      Away,
    Like to the summer's rain;
Or as the pearls of Morning's dew,
    Ne'er to be found again.

—Robert Herrick

Grape Sherbet

The Day? Memorial.
After the grill
Dad appears with his masterpiece—
swirled snow, gelled light.
We cheer. The recipe's
a secret and he fights
a smile, his cap turned up
so the bib resembles a duck.

That morning we galloped
through the grassed-over mounds
And named each stone
for a lost milk tooth. Each dollop
of sherbet, later,
is a miracle,
like salt on a melon that makes it sweeter.

Everyone agrees—it's wonderful!
It's just how we imagined lavender
would taste. The diabetic grandmother
stares from the porch,
a torch
of pure refusal.

We thought no one was lying
there under our feet,
we thought it
was a joke. I've been trying
to remember the taste,
but it doesn't exist.
Now I see why you bothered,
father.

—Rita Dove

Heart, have no pity on this house of bone:
Shake it with dancing, break it down with joy.
No man holds mortgage on it; it is your own;
To give, to sell at auction, to destroy.
When you are blind to moonlight on the bed,
When you are deaf to gravel on the pane,
Shall quavering caution from this house instead
Cluck forth at summer mischief in the lane?
All that delightful youth forbears to spend
Molestful age inherits, and the ground
Will have us; therefore, while we're young, my friend—
The Latin's vulgar, but the advice is sound.
Youth, have no pity; leave no farthing here
For age to invest in compromise and fear.

—Edna St. Vincent Millay

A Passing Glimpse

To Ridgely Torrence
on last looking into his "Hesperides"

I often see flowers from a passing car
That are gone before I can tell what they are.

I want to get out of the train and go back
To see what they were beside the track.

I name all the flowers I am sure they weren't;
Not fireweed loving where woods have burnt—

Not bluebells gracing a tunnel mouth—
Not lupine living on sand and drouth.

Was something brushed against my mind
That no one on earth will ever find?

Heaven gives its glimpses only to those
Not in a position to look too close.

—Robert Frost

Nothing Gold Can Stay

Nature's first green is gold,
Her hardest hue to hold.
Her early leaf's a flower;
But only so an hour.
Then leaf subsides to leaf.
So Eden sank to grief,
So dawn goes down to day.
Nothing gold can stay.

—Robert Frost

Lesson 32
Personal Response to Poetry

Objective
- To explore more ways of understanding poetry

Notes to the Teacher
The poems in this lesson carry writers a step further by encouraging them to select their favorite love poem to compare with the samples and analyze in similar fashion. Their discussions and written analyses can be assessed to determine their level of comprehension.

You might consider enlisting the help of the school media specialist in arranging to have a number of love poem collections available to students for browsing. Possibilities include

- *Emily Dickinson's Love Poems*
- *20 Love Poems and a Song of Despair*, Pablo Neruda
- *Great Love Poems*, ed. Shane Weller
- *A Book of Love Poetry*, ed. Jon Stallworthy
- *Love Poems: Everyman's Library Pocket Poets*, ed. Peter Washington
- *Contemporary's 100 Classic Love Poems*
- *Sonnets from the Portugese*, Elizabeth Barrett Browning

In addition, you might encourage students to consider the lyrics of various Top 40 love songs or Broadway musicals.

Procedure
1. Distribute **Handout 49**. After silent reading, ask for volunteers to read each poem in part A aloud.

   If any words other than the footnoted ones need explanation, give the requested information. The closing couplet of Shakespeare's sonnet is stated in a contrary-to-fact condition that may puzzle many students. The writer states a condition—something which is obviously not so—to emphasize how sure he is of what he says. It would be like saying, "If I'm making a mistake right now, then I'm a monkey's uncle."

2. Put the following general questions on the board or overhead and conduct a general discussion about the poems.

   a. What questions do you have about people in the poems? Who is the speaker? the person addressed? the person described? (*William Shakespeare's speaker is addressing his friend, Edna St. Vincent Millay's speaker is addressing her lover, Robert Frost's speaker is talking of a woman to a general reader, and Dorothy Parker is speaking to a general reader. A reader cannot assume that the speaker is the same person as the poet.*)

   b. What questions do you have about the setting? (*The speaker in Shakespeare's sonnet may have been sitting on a wharf watching a ship's first appearance on the horizon. Millay: after a night of lovemaking; Frost: field in summer; Parker: no setting.*)

   c. What images does each poem present? (*Shakespeare: Love as the north star is a fixed mark for sailors; ship; time as an old man with a sickle. Millay: meat; drink; slumber; roof; floating spar; blood; bones; man seeking death for lack of love. Frost: silken tent set in a field, swaying in breeze but firmly held to central pole. Parker: a soft, fragile, perfect rose*)

   d. How does Millay's sonnet compare with Shakespeare's? (*Both define love in negatives, what it is not. In Shakespeare's second quatrain, he changes to positive images, but then returns to negatives in the third quatrain. Both end with a hypothesis: Shakespeare is certain of the strength of love; Millay is doubtful, wonders whether she could sustain it in situations of great stress. Language in each is simple, direct.*)

   e. How does Frost differ from both? (*His speaker describes the woman in positive terms as a symbol of love. They only feel restrictive bonds very slightly—as a summer breeze tugs at the cords which hold the tent in place. A tent implies shelter but its looseness also allows all of earth to be loved and encompassed.*)

 f. How does Parker's treatment of her main image differ from that of the other poems? (*She treats a romantic image sardonically. She would prefer a display of riches to a display of endearment.*)

 g. Which poem means the most to you? Why? Did you find yourself agreeing or disagreeing with particular observations? Which ones?

3. Have students meet in the small groups formed during Lesson 31. Ask them to formulate their own questions about the poems as a prewriting activity.

4. Assign part B of **Handout 49** and the first draft of a comparison/contrast essay on the four poems. Tell writers that they may also consider personal questions of their own—questions to which they really do not know the answers.

5. Allow time for peer conferences within groups. Each writer should bring the selected love poem with analysis questions to discuss with peer groups. Peers may offer observations about similarities or differences between the personal selections and the four poems studied.

6. Ask students to complete their papers by adding their analysis of their favorite love poem and incorporate peer conferencing suggestions as they write a second draft of their comparison/contrast essays.

Students can meet in small groups to silently read each other's essays. Remind students to be alert for the following items:

- sentence fragments and run-ons
- correct capitalization, punctuation, and spelling
- subject-verb and pronoun-antecedent agreement

7. Set a due date for the final draft. **Handout 50,** an evaluation rubric, can be used to guide and assess student's essays.

Medley of Love

Part A.

Directions: Read the following love poems twice. The first time you read each one, try to get the general idea of who is saying what to whom—and how. The second time, think about common threads that run throughout all four poems. Stop to read the footnotes for any terms you do not recognize. Jot down any questions you have about the people, setting, or images, and be prepared for class discussion.

Sonnet 116

Let me not to the marriage of true minds
Admit impediments. Love is not love
Which alters when it alteration finds,
or bends with the remover to remove.
Oh no! It is an ever-fixéd mark
That looks on tempests and is never shaken.
It is the star[1] to every wandering bark[2]
Whose worth's unknown although his height[3] be taken.
Love's not Time's fool, though rosy lips and cheeks
Within his bending sickle's compass come.
Love alters not with his brief hours and weeks,
But bears it out even to the edge of doom.[4]
  If this be error and upon me proved,
  I never writ, nor no man ever loved.

—William Shakespeare

The Silken Tent

She is as in a field a silken tent
At midday when a sunny summer breeze
Has dried the dew and all its ropes relent,
So that in guys[5] it gently sways at ease,
And its supporting central cedar pole,
That is its pinnacle[6] to heavenward
And signifies the sureness of the soul,
Seems to owe naught to any single cord,
But strictly held by none, is loosely bound
By countless silken ties of love and thought
To everything on earth the compass round,
And only by one's going slightly taut
In the capriciousness of summer air
Is of the slightest bondage made aware.

—Robert Frost

[1]north star
[2]ship
[3]height of ship's mast
[4]judgment day
[5]ropes supporting the tent
[6]highest point

Love is not at all: it is not meat nor drink
Not slumber nor a roof against the rain;
Nor yet a floating spar to men that sink
And rise and sink and rise and sink again;
Love can not fill the thickened lung with breath,
Nor clean the blood, nor set the fractured bone;
Yet many a man is making friends with death
Even as I speak, for lack of love alone.
It well may be that in a difficult hour,
Pinned down by pain and moaning for release,
Or nagged by want past resolution's power,
I might be driven to sell your love for peace,
Or trade the memory of this night for food.
It well may be. I do not think I would.

—Edna St. Vincent Millay

One Perfect Rose

A single flow'r he sent me, since we met.
  All tenderly his messenger he chose;
Deep-hearted, pure, with scented dew still wet—
  One perfect rose.

I knew the language of the floweret;
  "My fragile leaves," it said, "his heart enclose."
Long love has taken for its amulet
  One perfect rose.

Why is it no one ever sent me yet
  One perfect limousine, do you suppose?
Ah no, it's always just my luck to get
  One perfect rose.

—Dorothy Parker

Part B.

Directions: Copy your choice of a modern love poem (or song) below.

Title: _____

Author: _____

Name _____

Date _____

Poetry Evaluation

Directions: Each of the following criteria will be given a score. Use this rubric as a guide while completing your assignment.

Criteria	Points	
1. The style and content are directed to the target audience.	_____	/8
2. The essay expresses and fulfills a purpose.	_____	/8
3. The writer presents and supports a main idea.	_____	/8
4. Each paragraph has a main idea.	_____	/8
5. All paragraphs are relevant.	_____	/8
6. Paragraphs are well-organized.	_____	/8
7. The conclusion is clearly stated.	_____	/8
8. The writer presents an effective comparison/contrast of		
a. speaker	_____	/8
b. setting	_____	/8
c. image	_____	/8
d. tone	_____	/8
e. mood	_____	/8
f. sound structure	_____	/8
9. The mechanics are correct.	_____	/8
10. There is sentence variety.	_____	/4
11. Action verbs are used.	_____	/4
12. Colorful, detailed language is used.	_____	/4
13. Word economy is used.	_____	/4
Total points	_____	/128

Comments:

Lesson 33
Critical Response to Poetry

Objectives
- To clarify a poem's meaning through critical response
- To write a more formal response to poetry

Notes to the Teacher

The study of two poems will give students practice in producing a more formal response to poetry, especially to poems which have a fair degree of difficulty. The study guide questions are to help the reader take an imaginary walk down a run-down neighborhood street in the middle of the night, noticing wretched objects, associating them with things in the past, and seeing it all as a reflection on the emptiness of modern life. The disillusionment of an idealist is a theme typical of T. S. Eliot.

When students finish their analysis, you might tell them that T. S. Eliot, as a child of a wealthy family, led a very sheltered life until he came to Harvard University. In his student days, his walks around Boston and Cambridge opened the door to a world which he had not known existed. He was moved by the desperate plight of the slum dwellers, and he was also frustrated by the shallow snobbery of the rich in his own social milieu. "Rhapsody on a Windy Night," a poem dwelling on this world, was written in 1910. *Old Possum's Book of Practical Cats*, a book of poetry he wrote for children, was published in 1939. In 1981, Trevor Nunn combined the whimsical elements of *Practical Cats* and the melancholy elements of "Rhapsody" to create the hit Broadway musical *Cats*. "Memory," the only poem not written by Eliot, has been the hit tune of the show. Nunn acknowledged that he drew his ideas for it from "Rhapsody." All the other songs in *Cats* are taken word for word from Eliot's book. Try to have at least one copy on hand for student perusal.

Procedure
1. Distribute **Handout 51**. Read the first poem in part A to the class.

2. If you have a tape or CD of the musical *Cats*, play the song "Memory" for the class.

If not, have a volunteer read it aloud. If any students have seen the show, have them offer their comments on it.

3. Have small groups complete part B. Explain that working together will help them brainstorm ideas, comments, and questions about the poems. Move from group to group and assist as needed. Discuss responses as a class.

Suggested Responses:

1. *In music, it indicates an irregular form, suggests improvisation technique. It can also mean exaggerated feeling or enthusiasm. The first applies to the poem since the tone is one of cool detachment, remembrances of distasteful things on a cold windy night.*

2. *run-down street in the city, between midnight and four o'clock in the morning*

3. *It is a sordid scene; reflecting upon it arouses disgust in the speaker, which governs his selection of details in his remembrance.*

4. *Classical poets identified the moon with the virgin goddess, Diana; moon and moonlight are usually pictured as enhancing a scene with beauty or as inspiring lovers. The speaker pictures the moon as a has-been prostitute.*

5. *All the disparate objects along the street are revealed in the moonlight.*

6. *Probably having a nightmare when the subconscious mind ignores the rationality of the conscious mind.*

7. *We feel its presence in the sputtering lamp, the whispered incantations. Wind is like a force that drives him along the unpleasant street.*

8. *possibly the speaker's interior reactions to what he sees and the connections he makes with the past*

9. *driftwood thrown on a beach; skeleton of the world; a broken rusted spring, brittle, and ready to snap in a factory yard*

10. the vacant-eyed child reaching for a toy, eyes peering out of shuttered windows, an old crab trying to grab a stick—all like things juxtaposed in a dream

11. See lines 52–61 and the response to question 4; underlying image of the moon like an old prostitute, withered, rejected, forgetful.

12. The memories recall dried out things— geraniums, dust; street smells— chestnuts, and smells of human left-overs—prostitutes, cigarettes, dregs of liquor.

13. Now the lamp guides the wanderer to his own house, his own reality.

14. If what he saw on this walk is a reflection of life, including his own, then his answer is "Thanks, but no thanks."

15. The lamp represents the irrational world of nightmare where conscious and unconscious impressions are intertwined.

16. The metric pattern is very irregular, iambic tetrameter broken by short gasping lines. The rhymes, too, are irregular, but have a harsh sound that fits the hard, dull scene of a city street.

4. Have small groups complete part C and share their responses. This activity may take more than one class period.

Suggested Responses:

1. Grizabella, the Glamour Cat

2. moonlit night in an alley

3. The speakers are different (a female cat in "Memory" and a male person in "Rhapsody"), but the settings are similar.

4. She has lost her memory, is smiling alone.

5. with gladness

6. Fatalistic warning reflects fatalistic drums; lamp gutters "but someone mutters" in "Memory"; in "Rhapsody," the lamp sputters and mutters.

7. Great note of hope: Grizabella the cat is hoping for her "ninth life."

8. Staleness of burnt out pleasures: See lines 60–69 in "Rhapsody."

9. Grizabella has hope of a better life. If the others touch her, they too will share the hope of happiness. In "Rhapsody," all the remembrances of disillusionment are themselves among life's cruelties. There is no hope.

10. Cats reflect humans in many ways. In the beginning they act as humans in judging Grizabella. Gradually, when they all meet to decide on who will get the ninth life, they suddenly see themselves in her and agree to old Deuteronomy's decision.

5. When all preliminary discussions are completed, assign part D. Allow two or three days for completion of a first draft.

6. Set days for conferencing the first and second drafts, editing, and handing in the final paper. **Handout 52,** an evaluation rubric, can be used to guide and assess students' essays.

Remembering: Poet's and Cat's Eye Views

Part A.

Directions: As you listen to T. S. Eliot's and Trevor Nunn's poems, try to visualize the night scenes and hear the tones of the speakers. Notice how sound patterns contribute to the mood of each poem. Be prepared to compare and contrast the poems.

Rhapsody on a Windy Night

Twelve o'clock.
Along the reaches of the street
Held in a lunar synthesis,
Whispering lunar incantations
Dissolve the floors of memory
And all its clear relations,
Its divisions and precisions,
Every street lamp that I pass
Beats like a fatalistic drum,
And through the spaces of the dark   10
Midnight shakes the memory
As a madman shakes a dead geranium.

Half-past one.
The street-lamp sputtered,
The street-lamp muttered,
The street-lamp said, "Regard that woman
Who hesitates toward you in the light of the
     door
Which opens on her like a grin.
You see the border of her dress   20
Is torn and stained with sand,
And you see the corner of her eye
Twists like a crooked pin."
The memory throws up high and dry
A crowd of twisted things:
A twisted branch upon the beach
Eaten smooth, and polished
As if the world gave up
The secret of its skeleton,
Stiff and white.   30
A broken spring in a factory yard,
Rust that clings to the form that the strength
has left
Hard and curled and ready to snap.

Half-past two,
The street-lamp said,
"Remark the cat which flattens itself in the gutter,
Slips out its tongue
And devours a morsel of rancid butter."
So the hand of the child, automatic,   40
Slipped out and pocketed a toy that was
running along the quay.
I could see nothing behind that child's eye.
I have seen eyes in the street
Trying to peer through lighted shutters

And a crab one afternoon in a pool,
An old crab with barnacles on his back,
Gripped the end of stick which I held him.

Half-past three,
The lamp sputtered,   50
The lamp muttered in the dark.
The lamp hummed:
"Regard the moon,
La lune ne garde aucune rancune
She winks a feeble eye,
She smiles into corners.
She smoothes the hair of the grass.
The moon has lost her memory.
A washed-out smallpox cracks her face,
Her hand twists a paper rose,   60
That smells of dust and eau de Cologne,
She is alone
With all the old nocturnal smells
That cross and cross across her brain."
The reminiscence comes of sunless dry geraniums
And dust in crevices,
Smells of chestnuts in the streets,
And female smells in shuttered rooms
And cigarettes in corridors
And cocktail smell in bars.   70
The lamp said,
"Here is the number on the door.
Memory!
You have the key,
The little lamp spreads a ring on the stair.
Mount.
The bed is open; the tooth-brush hangs on the wall,
Put your shoes at the door, sleep, prepare for life."
The last twist of the knife.   80

—T. S. Eliot

Memory

Midnight, not a sound from the pavement,
Has the moon lost her memory?
She is smiling alone.
In the lamp light the withered leaves collect
at my feet
And the wind begins to moan.

Memory. All alone in the moonlight
I can smile at the old days.
I was beautiful then.
I remember the time I knew what happiness   10
was,
Let the memory live again.

Every street lamp seems to beat a fatalistic
warning.
Someone mutters and the street lamp gutters,
And soon it will be morning.

Daylight. I must wait for the sunrise
I must think of a new life
And I mustn't give in.
When the dawn comes tonight will be a   20
memory, too
And a new day will begin.

Burnt out ends of smoky days,
The stale cold smell of morning.
The street lamp dies, another night is over.
Another day is dawning.

Touch me. It's so easy to leave me
All alone with the memory
Of my days in the sun.
If you touch me you'll understand what   30
happiness is.
Look, a new day has begun.

—Trevor Nunn

Part B.

Directions: Think critically about "Rhapsody on a Windy Night" as you answer the following questions on a separate sheet of paper.

1. Dictionaries give at least two meanings for the word *rhapsody.* What are they? Which one applies to this poem? How is this poem a "windy rhapsody?"

2. When and where is this poem set? How do you imagine the scene?

3. How is the setting important to the whole poem? Why has the poet chosen this particular setting as the backdrop? What atmosphere does the scene create? How does the speaker's mood match that atmosphere?

4. What do poets usually write about the moon or moonlight? What makes Eliot's response different?

5. How is the word *synthesis* used in line 3? What does it mean here?

6. The chants of the moon "dissolve the floors of memory." How would you describe the speaker's state of mind?

7. Wind is mentioned only in the title, not in the poem itself. What signs of the wind's presence do you find in the poem? What influence does it have on the speaker?

8. At the beginning of the second stanza, the street lamp does what a lamp could realistically do. But then it begins talking. What does the talking street lamp represent?

9. What contrasting images does the speaker remember?

10. In stanza three, the street lamp highlights a cat in the gutter. By association with this unreal turn in the poem, the speaker recalls three things. What are they?

11. In stanza four, note the sequence of the lamp's utterance—sputtered, muttered, hummed. The French line, "The moon does not bear any malice," leads to a detailed personification of the moon. Pick out the details. What is the central, underlying image? How does it differ from the usual image of the moon?

12. Each stanza is divided into two parts: one the speech of the lamp, the other the memories it arouses in the speaker. How do the memories in this stanza connect with the description of the moon?

13. In the last stanza, the lamp again marks the time of night. How do the words of the lamp differ from its earlier speeches?

14. Why does the speaker regard the last line of the lamp's speech as "the last twist of the knife"?

15. What might the speeches of the lamp represent? When might the speaker's—or anyone else's—thoughts and perceptions include such strange things as talking lamps?

16. What do you notice about the sounds in the poem as you hear it read aloud? How is the speaker feeling? How do the sound patterns match that person's state of mind?

Part C.

Directions: Think critically about "Memory" as you answer the following questions on a separate piece of paper.

1. Who is the speaker in this poem?

2. What is the setting?

3. How do these two elements compare and contrast with "Rhapsody on a Windy Night"?

4. What do both speakers say about the moon?

5. How does the speaker of this poem recall the past?

6. What images from "Rhapsody" are reflected in the third stanza? How do these images differ in the two poems?

7. Contrast the speakers in both poems. In stanza four, how is the tone and attitude different from that conveyed by the speaker in "Rhapsody"?

8. In stanza five, what do the memory images tell of the speaker's past? How do they echo images in "Rhapsody"?

9. What is the mood of the speaker in the last stanza? Compare and contrast it with the last lines of "Rhapsody."

10. In the musical *Cats*, when Grizabella, the Glamour Cat, first appears, the others all shrink from her. At her last appearance, all the cats gather around her and reach out to her as she sings her last lines. Can you think why Trevor Nunn arranged it that way?

Part D.

Directions: In both poems, there is an alternating pattern of seeing the present and remembering the past. The settings in both poems are similar. The action of walking alone on a moonlit night is the same, but the tones and attitudes of the speakers are somewhat different. In a two- to three-page paper, develop these ideas derived from your analysis using a comparison/contrast method. You may wish to use the following prewriting organizer and final form frame.

Similarities

Settings   _____

                    _____

Action   _____

                    _____

Wording   _____

                    _____

Other   _____

                    _____

Nunn Poem	Differences	Eliot Poem
_____	Speakers	_____
_____	Tone	_____
_____	Wording	_____
_____	Final thought	_____
_____	Other	_____

Frame

Paragraph 1—Introduction: general statements about the similarities and differences between the two poems

Paragraph 2—setting of poem A, setting of poem B

Paragraph 3—action of poem A, action of poem B

Paragraph 4—tone/attitudes of poem A, tone/attitude of poem B

Paragraph 5—ending of poem A, ending of poem B

Paragraph 6—Conclusion: interesting final thought on why Nunn took and changed what he did

Poetry Evaluation

Directions: Each of the following criteria will be given a score. Use this rubric as a guide while completing your assignment.

Criteria	Points
1. The style and content are directed to the target audience.	_____ /8
2. The essay expresses and fulfills a purpose.	_____ /8
3. The writer presents and supports a main idea.	_____ /8
4. Each paragraph has a main idea.	_____ /8
5. All paragraphs are relevant.	_____ /8
6. Paragraphs are well-organized.	_____ /8
7. The conclusion is clearly stated.	_____ /8
8. The writer presents an effective comparison/contrast of	
a. speaker	_____ /8
b. setting	_____ /8
c. image	_____ /8
d. tone	_____ /8
e. mood	_____ /8
f. sound structure	_____ /8
9. The mechanics are correct.	_____ /8
10. There is sentence variety.	_____ /4
11. Action verbs are used.	_____ /4
12. Colorful, detailed language is used.	_____ /4
13. Word economy is used.	_____ /4
Total points	_____ /128

Comments:

Lesson 34
Writing an Original Poem

Objectives
- To discover subjects for poetry in the everyday environment
- To use techniques that stimulate a writer's imagination

Notes to the Teacher
Having gained some personal insights from close reading of great poems, young writers may now enjoy writing their own. In previous lessons, prose models were used to inspire and provide forms for good writing. The model offered in this lesson was selected because it takes a fresh look at an otherwise nondescript scene and brings it to life. It is a workable, flexible model for students, and an exercise that can easily assess students' ability to brainstorm and develop subjects for poetry.

Procedure
1. Share as many of the following ideas as you judge appropriate for the class:

   Now that you have spent days reading, discussing, questioning, and writing about other people's poems, you may like to write one of your own. You have learned to find the meaning of a poem by examining it part by part and then fitting all the parts together. You asked and answered questions about major writers from William Shakespeare to Robert Frost. You noticed that when poets wrote about abstract ideas, such as love or time, they expressed their thoughts in very real, earthy images, like a tent in a field, a ship seen on the far horizon, or daffodils. They look at the same things we do, but they give them a fresh look, or use them to represent the unseen.

   You have seen that poets closely observe the world around them. They store up details to use later in their poems. Many writers carry a pocket-sized pad to record their first impressions of vivid image and events. Later, they shape those first impressions into a size and shape needed for the poem. Recall what the Greeks meant by *poet*—a craftsperson, one who deliberately fashions his or her thoughts in the most suitable form.

   A good place to start writing a poem is your own environment. Look around you. You don't have to have a great estate, a beautiful woodland scene, or the roar and rhythm of the tide at a beach. A city street, your own backyard, even your own room can provide images for poems. Brainstorm other everyday settings that could serve as subjects for poems.

2. Distribute **Handout 53**. Tell students that May Swenson looks very closely at her world, notes sharp details, and transforms them into poetic images. Have students read the poem silently. If you wish, you may have the class read it aloud as a choral reading. At each change of verb, have a new speaker read the lines.

3. Divide the class into small groups formed during Lesson 31, and have them answer the questions on the handout. Allow about ten minutes for discussion.

4. Tell the class they may do the next step of this exercise alone or with the group. Ask for suggestions for new topics that could be developed in the same way Swenson developed sunset (sunrise, moonlight, snow, rain, wind, music).

5. Direct students to draft their poems in class, rework them at home, and bring them to class the next day for conferencing and more drafting. Students who need a more structured task might be told to use May Swenson's poem as a model. Supply them with the following frame.

   a. Choose some weather change as your topic.

   b. Imagine how that weather changes the world around you.

   c. Picture the before and after. Follow the weather change in your imagination from one place to another (or from one moment to the next).

   d. Brainstorm at least ten before-and-after details.

e. Brainstorm at least ten vivid verbs that describe the actions you see around you as the weather change occurs. These will be the first words of most lines in your poem.

f. Draft your poem as one long sentence.

g. Add colorful describing words that tell how the setting looks, sounds, tastes, smells, and feels. (Use a dictionary or thesaurus to find interesting words.)

h. Remove any unnecessary words.

i. Play with different line breaks; read each version aloud and see which you prefer.

6. When the poems are ready for publishing, have volunteers arrange these "word pictures" on the bulletin board. If you wish, use the following checklist to assess students' ability to understand and use techniques for stimulating the imagination.

"Word Picture" Poem Checklist

____ a. The subject and action are clear.

____ b. The place described is the writer's nearby environment.

____ c. Strong pictures are created in the listener's mind.

____ d. Changes are vividly described.

____ e. Colorful, unusual, or even made-up verbs are used.

____ f. Descriptive adjectives are used.

____ g. Sounds and ideas flow when read aloud.

____ h. The poem shows that the writer used his or her imagination.

Poem for Practice

Directions: As you read May Swenson's poem about sunset, note how she describes an ordinary scene in a very extraordinary way. Then answer the questions that follow.

Ornamental Sketch with Verbs

Sunset runs in a seam
over the brows of buildings
  dropping west to the river,
turns the street to a gilded stagger,
makes the girl on skates,
  the man with the block of ice,
  the basement landlady calling her cat
  creatures in a dream.

scales with salamander-red
  the window-pitted walls,
hairs the gutters with brindled light,
helmet cars and boys on bikes

and double-dazzles
  the policeman's portly coat,
halos the coal truck where
  nuggets race from a golden sled,

festoons lampposts to fantastic trees,
lacquers sooty roofs and pavements,
floats in every puddle
  pinks of cloud,
flamingos all the pigeons,
grands all dogs to chows,
enchants the ash cans into urns
  and fire-escapes to Orleans balconies.

—May Swenson

1. How many sentences are there in this poem?

2. What is the subject?

3. List all the verbs.

4. List the unusual verbs (words not commonly used as verbs) used by Swenson.

5. Use a colored pen, pencil, or highlighter to mark each main verb, its object, and all modifiers in alternate colors. For example, use red for the first, black for the second, and blue for the third.

6. Consult a dictionary and explain how these words say just what the poet wants: *brindled, chows, flamingos, lacquers, salamander.*

Part 8
Across the Curriculum

Interdisciplinary approaches can enable students to improve writing. Students often need explicit instruction in how to apply their general understanding of the writing process to the specific task of writing an article or paper for a science or history class. The lessons in Part 7 were based on the belief that students need direct instruction to transfer what they already know about prewriting, drafting, conferencing, revising, editing, and publishing to a particular writing task: responding to literature. Such explicit instruction is probably even more vital for learning to write successfully in the various subject areas, yet it is often a type of instruction for which subject area teachers feel they have too little time or training.

Among prewriting activities, research—including formal library research—plays a key role in this type of writing. As Lesson 36 stresses, accuracy is essential. These four lessons, which use the U.S. prohibition amendment and the bombing of Japan in World War II as examples, make a direct transfer of the six-activity writing process to American history. Allow substantial drafting time between Lessons 36 and 37, as well as for revision between Lessons 37 and 38.

Lesson 35
A Social Studies Application

Objective
* To select a social studies topic and a writing mode

Notes to the Teacher
One skill can reap many successes. Facility with the writing process is transferable from English composition to other disciplines; students should now see positive results in their papers for other subjects. Many students begin to value the writing process more as they recognize its adaptability to assignments in various classes. For many students, pride in writing skill intensifies when they discover that a teacher besides their English teacher admires their writing. When they succeed in producing quality compositions in other classes, they start to view themselves as "writers."

The completion of this assignment allows assessment of students' ability to select and design writing topics in other disciplines. It presents the following options to teachers and students:

a. Direct students to write a social studies essay on an assigned topic or a topic of their choice.

b. Collaborate with the social studies teacher, who will provide background and direct students' research while the composition teacher supervises the writing process.

c. Permit students to choose their topic, select a writing mode, and conduct research. This is a good time to reacquaint students with the library.

d. The two topics provided in this unit (Prohibition and the dropping of the atomic bomb) both emphasize history as decisions, and not as fate—a perspective that makes history less tidy and more relevant to our present political decisions.

e. Note that the types of prewriting activities students choose will depend on the writing mode that is assigned or selected. A student writing a mock autobiographical piece from the point of view of someone who lived through Prohibition, for example, might want to interview some senior citizens; a student writing an argumentative piece that criticizes Truman's decision to drop the bombs, on the other hand, might engage in a prewriting debate with classmates. While the procedures specifically relate to a social studies essay, they can be altered for use with any topic in any discipline.

Procedure
1. Tell students that over the next few lessons they will be choosing a topic for a social studies essay, researching that topic, and writing an essay on it. You should specify an approximate length that is appropriate for your class and time constraints. Point out that this is not the typical enormous, daunting "research paper" assignment with which they may be familiar. It is a process writing assignment—like those they have been doing throughout the unit—broken into manageable pieces. It is also an assignment that enables them to become actively involved in gathering information about something that interests them.

2. If you have decided to limit the topics to Prohibition and dropping the atomic bomb on Japan, write these on the board or overhead. Have students brainstorm their previous knowledge about each as you jot down their ideas.

If you have not decided to limit the topics, try to elicit some other possibilities from students and note these on the board or overhead. To stimulate ideas, you might suggest that they think of key decisions or approaches to big problems that altered the course of history in some way. Encourage them to consider issues that really interest them, and how those issues have affected them. Remind them that their fellow students will be the audience for the report, so it should also be about a topic they think other students would want to know more about.

3. Unless you have decided that everyone will do independent research, tell students that they have a choice of collaboration with a partner or small group or doing the research on their own.

4. Remind students that over the course of this writing unit, they have done a variety of types of writing. Ask students to recall these (*autobiography, narration, problem/solution, description, exposition, persuasion, argumentation*).

5. Point out that any of these approaches could be applied to the social studies essay they are about to write. Have students brainstorm examples of this and jot these on the board or overhead.

6. Ask students to select topics and writing modes, and to list at least ten questions they have about their topic. If the research is going to be a collaborative effort, these questions could later be divided among the team members.

Sample:

Mode	Topic—Prohibition	Topic—Atomic Bomb Dropping
Autobiography	member of the anti-saloon league	pilot on Enola Gay
Narrative	Izzy and Moe	a Hiroshima survivor
Problem/ Solution	How to curb excessive drinking (present-day or early twentieth-century point of view) 1. high alcohol taxes 2. education 3. alcohol revulsion pill (Antabuse)	How to end World War II, Pacific Theatre 1. land invasion of Japan 2. continue sea blocking 3. atomic or conventional bombing of Tokyo
Descriptive	speakeasy	Hiroshima or Nagasaki, the day after
Expository	Why the Eighteenth Amendment	Why Hiroshima and Nagasaki were chosen
Persuasive	letter to state legislature, urging ratification of Nineteenth Amendment	letter to President Truman urging him not to drop the bomb
Argumentative	Government should not legislate our eating and drinking habits.	Nuclear weapons should never be used.

Lesson 36
Research

Objective
- To research chosen topics

Notes to the Teacher
This lesson presumes students are conducting independent research or are focusing on one of the two topics provided in the previous lesson. If you are collaborating with another teacher, this lesson may be skipped. Students' research aptitude can be assessed through **Handout 54** and the bibliography cards that pertain to it.

Topic research will depend on the writing mode, the student's questions, and the availability of resources in the school or local library. Consider writing to community members who experienced Prohibition and/or World War II to address students.

Before students begin their research, you may wish to alert the media specialist and provide a list of topics so that he or she can help students find the items needed. You may also wish to review how to create bibliography cards (including those for electronic sources) and how to take notes on note cards.

Procedure
1. Have students share questions in small groups or as a class. Encourage them to note other questions they like, but also to recognize the value of their own questions. Students should learn to trust their own curiosity, and not rely exclusively on the opinions of experts.

2. Provide background information on Prohibition and the dropping of the atomic bomb. If students have seen *The Untouchables* or have read John Hersey's *Hiroshima*, discuss them. You may want to show the video *Decision to Drop the Bomb*.

3. Emphasize that the papers must be historically accurate in all details. The papers should incorporate primary and secondary sources, which must be cited at the end of the paper. Review how to create bibliography cards and explain that you will collect these for credit before students begin their first drafts.

4. Allow students some time to go to the library/media center. Remind them that they must carefully summarize their findings in their own words, because they will not be bringing the actual resources back to class when they draft their essays. You may choose to go as a group and to offer group instruction/individual help to students.

5. Have students complete **Handout 54** and hand in bibliography cards.

Optional Activity
Share with students the introductions on the Teacher Resource Page.

Sample Introductions

1. Topic: Prohibition

    Mode: Expository

    Many prohibitionists had good intentions: they wanted husbands, especially newly arrived immigrant ones, to spend less time and money in the saloons and more on their families. This "noble experiment" that started well-intentioned in 1920 nonetheless grew unmanageable by 1933. For one, many cultures, especially Jewish and Catholic, never viewed alcohol as evil but saw it as part of their tradition. They never supported the 18th Amendment. Another reason involved an understaffed Bureau of Prohibition that offered minimal resistance to the well-financed gangs and bootleggers. Finally, political strength started shifting to the urban Democrats who, unlike Republicans and rural Democrats, preferred "wet" to "dry."

2. Topic: Prohibition

    Mode: Autobiography

    I hated to break the news to him. He hadn't been in New York for more than twelve hours, and I could see he was getting thirsty.

    "Kevin," I explained to my twenty-one-year-old cousin, "It's not so easy. Didn't they tell you back home? Buying alcohol is against the law here in America."

    "Well that's a foin law, Jimmy," he said, standing up and rolling up his sleeves in irritation. "What koin of nonsense Jimmy, got into the head of these folks?"

    "That's just the way it is, Kevin. You'll get used to it."

    He looked at me as though I had sprouted ten heads. "Get used to it? Well let me tell you this, Jimmy. If the spirits were good enough for me father, and me grandfather, and me great-grandfather, and all the way back to the good Lord Himself, then they're good enough for Kevin McCafferty."

    There was no talking sense to him. I knew of the speakeasy on Fourth, and when I told Kevin about it, he grabbed his coat.

    "Now I feel welcome in America. Let's be takin' a walk that way."

3. Topic: Dropping the Atomic Bomb

    Mode: Argumentative

    No country, especially the United States, wants to use atomic bombs. Their capacity for destruction far exceeds that of conventional weaponry. The two atomic bombs dropped on Japan in 1945 killed 120,000 people instantly, and thousands more over the next forty years. Though it was a terrible moment in world history, I believe President Truman made the right decision to use the bombs for these reasons: 1) The decision saved the lives of many American soldiers who were battling an indomitable enemy; 2) the bomb permitted the United States to determine peace negotiations with Japan without bargaining with Russia; and 3) the Japanese did not respond to the ultimatum of surrender issued at the Potsdam Conference.

Name _____

Date _____

Prewriting

Part A.

Directions: Write five questions about your topic that you are really interested in answering.

Question	Source 1	Source 2	Source 3
1.			
2.			
3.			
4.			
5.			

Part B.

Directions: Find several primary and secondary sources that contain information on at least one of your questions. Consult at least one electronic source, if possible. After completing numbered bibliography cards for each source, complete the chart in part A with key findings. Extend the chart on another piece of paper, if necessary. Finally, collect the information in more detail on notecards.

Lesson 37
Drafting and Getting Feedback

Objectives

- To use research to write a first draft

- To respond to other students' essays and summarize others' responses

Notes to the Teacher

At this point, students know the components of a quality composition: specific audience, purpose, and topic; unified and organized paragraphs; concise and colorful language.

However, history compositions—in contrast with some other kinds of writing—must answer this question: Do the facts of this paper correspond with those we know are true? Since students are not drawing from personal experience nor arguing mainly from logic, their papers must be grounded in historical facts. Speakeasies should look like speakeasies; the atomic bomb was dropped on Hiroshima and not Hirohito. Students must also be able to answer this question: How do I know these facts are true? Are my sources credible? This is especially important in a time when anyone can claim anything on the Internet. Authenticity and accountability are paramount for a quality history composition.

Procedure

1. Explain that students will be using the information from **Handout 54** and from their notecards to write the first drafts of their papers. Specify the span of time for drafting (e.g., three days) and explain how much of the drafting will be done in class. Most of the drafting could be done in class (especially if this is a collaborative project) or students could be encouraged to work on individual writing tasks at home while communicating with each other either by getting together at someone's house or phoning each other.

2. Distribute **Handout 55,** the social studies evaluation form and discuss its contents so that everyone knows how the finished papers will be evaluated.

3. Allow students time to work on their drafts as you circulate and give help where needed. This is an opportune time to assess students' ability to respond to peer essays. If students have done group research, you might suggest that students follow this sequence:

   - Organize and compare the information each student has researched.

   - Decide on a thesis statement.

   - Decide how to organize the material.

   - Work independently on each piece.

   - As a group, revise pieces to make sure they all support the thesis and have a consistent tone.

   - Draft essay.

   Stress that during drafting, students will be selectively sifting information, including only that which supports the thesis. They may find that they need to revise their thesis. If this is a group project, they also may find, that one members' piece no longer fits the thesis. If this happens, reassure them that they will receive credit for their research (based on notecards and **Handout 54**) whether or not the information makes its way into the final paper.

4. When drafts are completed, direct students who have worked independently on the same writing mode (e.g., autobiography) to get into groups. Have groups use **Handout 56** as a guide for a conferencing session on each member's paper. When listening to responses, each student should complete **Handout 56** with specific comments about his or her own paper. (If this has been a group research project, the group could conference on each member's piece of the final paper.)

5. Direct students to incorporate peer suggestions as they revise their essays. Set a date for second drafts.

Name _____

Date _____

Social Studies Evaluation

Directions: Each of the following crtieria will be given a score. Use the rubric as a guide while completing your assignment.

Criteria	Points	
1. The style and content are suited to target audience.	_____	/8
2. The essay expresses and fulfills a purpose.	_____	/8
3. The essay is historically accurate.	_____	/8
4. The essay contains verifiable research.	_____	/8
5. Bibliographic material is properly cited.	_____	/8
6. The essay answers its own questions.	_____	/8
7. The writer demonstrates knowledge of the subject.	_____	/8
8. The writer works within the framework of selected mode.	_____	/8
9. The essay keeps to a specific topic.	_____	/8
10. The essay contains supporting ideas.	_____	/8
11. Each paragraph has a main idea.	_____	/8
12. All paragraphs are well-organized.	_____	/8
13. Transitions are smooth.	_____	/8
14. The conclusion is clearly stated.	_____	/8
15. The mechanics are correct.	_____	/4
16. There is sentence variety.	_____	/4
17. Action verbs are used.	_____	/4
18. Colorful, detailed language is used.	_____	/4
19. Word economy is used.	_____	/4
Total Points	_____	/132

Comments:

A Conference Checklist

Directions: As readers respond to your paper, check off the criteria you have fulfilled, summarize comments about your composition, and evaluate your peer conferencing experience.

Paper Title: _____

Peer Editors: _____

1. Criteria for all papers

   _____a. accurate historical facts   _____d. a specific, focused topic

   _____b. sources cited   _____e. ample detail that supports the topic

   _____c. a clear purpose and audience

2. Criteria for autobiography, anecdote, and narrative papers

   _____a. authentic historical atmosphere   _____c. action/dialogue

   _____b. conveys a characters thoughts
   and feelings

3. Criteria for descriptive papers

   _____a. specific setting   _____c. sensory language

   _____b. vivid details

4. Criteria for expository, problem/solution, persuasive, and argumentative papers

   _____a. clearly stated main ideas   _____c. sound logic/analogy

   _____b. paragraphs supporting main   _____d. convincing argument
   ideas

5. What are the strong points of the composition?

6. What are some suggestions for improvement?

7. What aspect of peer conferencing was most helpful? least helpful? Describe your experience with the peer conferencing process.

Lesson 38
Editing

Objectives

- To practice editing for common errors

- To edit one's own composition

Notes to the Teacher

This lesson presents a comprehensive checklist for editing. Students should use it as a guide to improvement, not view it as a punitive tool. If a student finds a couple of fragments while editing a partner's paper, for instance, he or she should simply note on the checklist where the problems are. The writer then edits the paper, fixes any problems, and checks off all fifteen points on the list. Students who need practice fixing the types of grammar, usage, and mechanics errors on the checklist can complete **Handout 58**. Both handouts are excellent tools for assessing students' capability for self-editing common errors.

Procedure

1. Instruct students to pair up, read each other's papers, and complete **Handout 57**, part A.

   Explain that the handout is a guide to help them find and correct "G.U.M." (grammar, usage, and mechanics) errors as well as weaknesses in content and structure (lack of supporting evidence, disorganized paragraphs).

2. Assign **Handout 58** if students need practice in identifying and correcting G.U.M. errors.

Suggested Responses:

The conquest of England by the Normans was not one of those conquests that results in the slavery of the conquered and leaves a gulf between two races—master and slave. That was the case in France, and resulted, after centuries of oppression, in the revolution of 1793, which shook not only France but the whole civilized world. Most of the population of England has been always free. People could intermarry into the ranks above them; they could sink into the ranks below them. Anyone acquainted with the origin of our English surnames may verify this fact for himself by looking at the names of a single street of shops. There, jumbled together, he will find names marking the noblest Saxon of Angle blood—Kenward, Kenric, Osgood, or Osborne—side by side with Cordery or Banister or other Norman-French names. The old blood-feud between Norseman and Englishman, between the descendants of those who conquered and those who were conquered, ended a long time ago. Proof is the fact that in the children of the Prince of Wales, eight hundred years later, the blood of William of Normandy is mingled with the blood of the very Harold who fell at Hastings.

3. Have students edit their own papers and complete part B of **Handout 57**.

4. Assign a due date for final drafts. Remind students to use the evaluation rubric on **Handout 55** (Lesson 37) as a guide for their final drafts.

Name _____

Date _____

Final Editing Checklist

Part A.

Directions: Read your partner's paper and complete the "Editor" column of the checklist. If you find any errors, briefly explain them in the space provided.

Title: _____

Writer: _____

Editor: _____

Editor	Writer	Criteria	Notes
_____	_____	1. No run-ons	
_____	_____	2. No fragments	
_____	_____	3. Correct capitalization	
_____	_____	4. Correct spelling	
_____	_____	5. Proper subject-verb agreement	
_____	_____	6. Proper pronoun-antecedent agreement	
_____	_____	7. Other G.U.M.	
_____	_____	8. Sentence variety	
_____	_____	9. Action verbs in active voice	
_____	_____	10. Colorful detailed language	
_____	_____	11. Concise sentences	
_____	_____	12. Clearly stated main ideas	
_____	_____	13. Supporting evidence	
_____	_____	14. Well-organized paragraphs	
_____	_____	15. Appropriate transitions	
_____	_____	16. Properly cited bibliographic material	
_____	_____	17. Other:	

Part B.

Directions: Read your own paper and complete the "Writer" column of the checklist. If you find any errors, briefly explain them in the space provided.

Name _____

Date _____

Identifying and Correcting Errors

Directions: Read the paragraph below about the Norman Conquest and use the final editing checklist to edit it for grammar, usage, and mechanics. You will find at least ten errors. Write the corrected paragraph in the space provided.

The conquest of England by the normans were not one of those conquests that results in the slavery of the conquered and leaves a gulf between two races—master and slave. That being the case in France, and resulted, after centuries of oppression, in the revolution of 1793. Shaking not only France but the whole civilized world. Most of the population of England, has been always free. They could intermarry into the ranks above them they could sink into the ranks below them. Anyone acquainted with the origin of our English surnames may verify this fact for themselves by looking at the names of a single street of shops. Their, jumbled together, he will find names marking the noblest Saxon of Angle blood—Kenward Kenric Osgood or Osborne—side by side with Cordery or Banister or other Norman-French names. The old blood-feud between Norseman and Englishman between the descendents of those who conquered and those who were conquered ended a long time ago. Proof is the fact that in the children of the Prince of Wales, 800 years later, the blood of William of Normandy is mingeled with the blood of the very Harold who fell at hastings.

Part 9
The Student Writer

Throughout this book, the importance of self-direction and ownership during the writing process has been stressed. These final two lessons offer culminating activities which reinforce that process-awareness.

The six-activity writing process is not peculiar to the classroom. As professional writers talk about their work, certain writing process elements inevitably surface. On the other hand, writers work very differently. Few take every piece of writing through a rigid six-step sequence. Fortunately the writing process is as adaptable as writers are idiosyncratic. Student writers are encouraged to consider how they have individualized the process.

This section offers an arena for students to devise and carry out their own writing projects. The reins are placed entirely in the writers hands, as they determine mode, topic, and audience. They also design prewriting approaches, conferencing opportunities, and revising and editing focuses. Finally, they seek appropriate publication channels.

Lesson 39
Personalizing the Writing Process

Objectives

- To examine how several professional writers use the writing process

- To describe common and unique student approaches to the process

Notes to the Teacher

While the writing process used throughout this unit stresses six universal stages, each writer shapes it to suit individual preferences and idiosyncracies. Students need to be aware of specific strategies and approaches that have proved valuable. Growth in awareness of one's personal composition process forms a foundation for confidence and success in future writing. The handouts in this lesson can assess that awareness.

Handout materials in this lesson are taken from various past issues of *Writing!* magazine. You may be interested in ordering this magazine for your students. Contact the Weekly Reader Corporation, (1–800–446–3355; http://www.weeklyreader.com).

Students interested in finding out how particular writers go about writing may enjoy looking up interviews with those writers on the Web, or reading *Speaking for Ourselves* and *Speaking for Ourselves, Too,* books of autobiographical sketches by notable authors of young adult literature that were compiled and edited by Donald R. Gallo.

Procedure

1. Remind students that the writing process they have been using incorporates six general recursive activities: prewriting, drafting, conferencing, revising, editing, and publishing. Writers often find themselves circling back through these activities—visiting and revisiting certain ones—as they write. They may repeat certain activities and skip others. They have probably noticed that some strategies work better for them than other techniques. For example, some writers prefer drafting by hand to drafting on the computer; some find it more beneficial to read their writing aloud before revising.

2. Have students complete **Handout 59**. Consider dividing the class into small groups and assigning each group a part of the handout. Discuss responses as a class. Ask students to compare and contrast each author's writing process.

Suggested Responses:

Part A.

1. *reading, interviews, research, reflecting*

2. *drafting followed by self-conferencing and revision to complete the paragraph before going to the rest of the essay*

3. *constant revision approach*

4. *leaving time (a day) between final revision and editing*

Part B.

1. *relating incidents to one another based on their common universal values*

2. *Words carry meaning as boats carry cargo; words are frail, rough, and as vulnerable as "tiny little boats" in a wide sea.*

3. *Without thorough revision, writing is not complete.*

Part C.

1. *reflecting on past experiences; creating imaginative transformations; keeping a journal; observing details; research*

2. *His topics are universal elements, and therefore have a wide appeal.*

3. *attention to word choice and organization*

3. Have partners complete **Handout 60**, taking turns as interviewer and interviewee. Encourage interviewers to devise questions to expand and clarify answers, and to record careful, accurate notes.

4. Ask volunteers to share their variations on the writing process such as always using a pencil, or self-conferencing and revision followed by peer conferencing and revision.

5. Have students keep the handout describing their personal process of writing.

Writers on Writing

Part A.

Directions: Read the following interview with Charles Leroux, a journalist who wrote essays and articles on a variety of subjects for the *Chicago Tribune,* and answer the four questions. Be prepared for class discussion.

Interviewer: Where do you find ideas?

Charles Leroux: A lot come from reading. For instance I read an ad in the *Texas Monthly* for spices for the chili that won more awards than any other chili in Texas. I called the chef because I thought it would be interesting to write about a man who started up a small business with a product that is of interest to almost everybody. Everybody feels strongly about chili. Well, when I talked to him, he was a lot better than I had imagined because he'd evolved this persona, this chili-persona of a crochety, old prospector. He wore a faded denim shirt, cowboy hat, and boots. He called himself Chili Lee in this role, while in "real life" he was Ed Patzel, a personnel director at the Hyatt House in Houston.

Interviewer: Can you think of an example of one story idea growing into another?

Charles Leroux: One time I thought it would be fun to do an article about a young physicist working in Princeton at the same place where Einstein used to work. But the more I talked to my subject, the more my story evolved into an answer to the question: "What's it like to have a job that no one understands?" This young physicist researches gravitational relativity, and absolutely nobody knows what that means. At parties he tells people he's an astronomer, but they think he says "an astrologer" and that causes even more problems.

Interviewer: How do you research a large subject, such as your recent feature on drunk driving?

Charles Leroux: I have made calls all over the country and gathered material from all over. For a broad subject like this, I start by making a list of sources. I might start with the *Readers' Guide to Periodical Literature* to find articles. Then I'll add to the list other sources, such as the National Safety Council, which has all of the accident statistics. As I begin talking to people, I'll always ask, "Who else should I talk to?" That's how I got the name of Dr. Paul Meyer, who is head of the spinal cord unit at Northwestern Hospital. He sees mostly people who have been paralyzed by automobile accidents. Things are usually very easy once you get to the right people.

Interviewer: How do you focus your ideas?

Charles Leroux: To do (a feature on) something like drunk driving, you have to think of some new aspect. It's not a new subject by any means, so you have to think of a way of presenting it that's different. I focused on public and private attitudes and how the lack of any kind of consensus about it makes it a problem that is unlikely to get solved. The article about Alzheimer's disease was different because no one had written about it except in the scientific press. But, of course, each installment had to have a definite focus.

Interviewer: How do you get started after you've come up with the idea and after you've completed your research?

Charles Leroux: I'll sit down and write a first paragraph, and then I'll look at it for what seems a week. It takes a long time to get started, but there's a good reason: once you get the first paragraph just right, then the next one follows and the next one follows after that. I can sense when things are working. I might have to go back and change the first paragraph, and then that might make me want to change the second one. In a sense, my articles are in a state of constant revision.

Interviewer: Do you have any editing tips?

Charles Leroux: I try never to turn in a story the same day I have been working on it. I let it sit overnight, and I make an effort not to think about it. When I look at it the next day I see all kinds of mistakes that just weren't there the day before.

Interviewer: What kinds of mistakes?

Charles Leroux: Mostly stupid things—grammatical mistakes, awkward constructions. Sometimes I'll find that I've used the same word twice in the same sentence, even though I've read that sentence over and over the day before.[1]

1. What prewriting activities does Charles Leroux customarily use?

2. Explain his method of composing the first paragraph.

3. How do his comments illustrate the recursive nature of writing?

4. Identify his main editing tip. Is this suggestion helpful to you? Why or why not?

[1]Robert Boone, "An Interview with Charles Leroux," *Writing!* (March 1984), 13–14.

Part B.

Directions: Maya Angelou, one of America's foremost contemporary writers, is best known for her autobiographies, beginning with the celebrated *I Know Why the Caged Bird Sings.* She has also written poetry and television scripts. Read the following interview, and answer the questions. Be prepared for class discussion.

Interviewer: When you write an autobiography, how do you decide which details and experiences to include and which to leave out?

Maya Angelou: Let me begin by saying that I have no precedent for what I'm trying to do with the autobiographical form. I'm the only writer in this country who says that my major work will be through this form. After my first book, I realized that this was the form that I really wanted to investigate. The autobiographer looks at life through the lens of his or her own life and really uses herself or himself as the jumping-off place to examine the social mores and the economic political climates. In a way, the autobiography becomes history as well as the story of one person, for it becomes the story of a family or the story of a state or nation.

Interviewer: But a person has so many experiences in the course of a lifetime. How did you decide which of your experiences to treat in your autobiographies?

Maya Angelou: Every human being's life is larger than any book or even twenty books. For my autobiographies I've chosen to concentrate on the broader subjects, such as greed, generosity, sloth, responsibility, love, and so on. Then, I've looked through my life for the period that I'm writing about, and I've found an incident that has encompassed that particular emotion.

Interviewer: Can you give an example of this process?

Maya Angelou: If a young person is writing about her experience in summer camp, where she encountered some hostility from some of the other campers, she has to paint those experiences on a broader canvas by trying to think of other times when she had been rejected by her peers. When she does that, she might discover that it isn't the camp story that she wants to tell, but the story about moving to a new neighbor-hood, instead. The story becomes one about rejection, and it includes some of the feelings from camp and some from the move to a new school as the writer chooses the best stories in which rejection is demon-strated. Then the writer works to tell that story so clearly that the reader is right there with her.

Interviewer: I would imagine that the process of writing an autobiography is both painful and cathartic. Did you find it to be so?

Maya Angelou: Well, you're right on the first score. It was painful. I haven't found it to be cathartic, however. Writing an autobiography is very painful, but it's gratifying, too. There's nothing so gratifying to me as to write well and to say almost what I mean. I say "almost" because I've never been able to say exactly what I mean. It is, after all, very difficult to take something as flimsy and frail as words and treat them as if they were tiny little boats, put meaning into them, and send them out to another human being. It's very difficult to have that other person understand exactly what I mean.

Interviewer: What advice can you give to young writers?

Maya Angelou: One of the problems we've had in this country recently is that young people have been told that they are poets and that all they need to do is be black or angry or in love and that if they let it all hang out, that is poetry. That is the worst thing that young people could learn, since what results most often is not poetry, but stream-of-consciousness gibberish. Putting down on paper what you have to say is an important part of writing, but the words and ideas have to be shaped and cleaned, cleaned as severely as a dog cleans a bone, cleaned until there's not a shred of anything superfluous. I know that it's hard to cut away at your own writing, but it's not really writing until you pare it down![2]

1. Describe Maya Angelou's prewriting process.

2. Explain her use of the "little boats" analogy.

3. How much emphasis does she place on the revision stage of the writing process?

[2]Gail Steinberg, "An Interview with Maya Angelou," *Writing!* (September 1982), 11–13.

Part C.

Directions: Read the following interview with playwright and children's writer Alan Gross, who began his career in advertising. Then answer the three questions that follow. Be prepared for class discussion.

Interviewer: What advice would you give to young writers?

Alan Gross: I would tell young writers to work on their stories and worry about putting them in the media later. Make sure your story is terrific. Make sure your characters are wonderful. Every time you go to a writing seminar, you are told to write what you know about. But no one teaches you how to figure out what you know. My method, and my idea and my philosophy, is how to parenthesize what you know. Try to figure out the places you have been in your life, the little incidents that have happened to you, and the little stories that have happened to you. Yes, of course, you haven't fought wars and you haven't fought bulls. You still have had an incident where your grandmother lived next to an old lady who did such and such. That's where the story comes from. William Saroyan, who died about two years ago, wrote a very charming little book called *Places Where I Have Done Time.* All he did was figure out all the places he had been—hotels, houses, jobs, grandmothers' houses—and just made two- and three-page notes on everything. That was the whole book, a hundred little vignettes. That's where you start. You take a guy from here, a time from there.

Interviewer: Then where does reality fit in? Is it a starting point?

Alan Gross: Sure it's a starting point. I'll give you an example. This is the project I am doing right now as we speak. It is called *The Conversation of Leo Novotny.* It is about my grandfather who had a little store on Kedzie Avenue in the 50's and about the man who owned the store next to him in which revival meetings were held. My grandfather's name was not Leo Novotny. His name was Leo Gross. Novotny was the name of the family who lived upstairs from us when we were kids. I took this story from one little incident that happened. It's not like I was in Vietnam and my leg got blown off, that big story. It's a little story, explored and heightened and changed and worked on through the artistic process.

Interviewer: You think of possibilities, then, arising from one actual event.

Alan Gross: You see where it goes and what would make it work better. The character of Leo Novotny is vaguely based upon my grandfather. The character of Daniel Madison, the reverend, is based on a bus driver whom I did a story on for *Chicago* magazine. I'm into journalism, too. So I am out there with my pad and my tape recorder and I am seeing things. There are things out there to see.

Interviewer: Do you keep a journal to record the things you see?

Alan Gross: I did and I recommend it to people. Write your journal but don't write diaries. Don't write, "Today I talked to Susie." I would rather have you write bon mots. For instance, today I had breakfast at a cafe on Lincoln Avenue. One grill man turned to another grill man who was lighting up a cigarette and said, "You've got time to lean, you've got time to clean." And that just struck up visions of a charming time when I was a young hot-dog slinger in Skokie, Illinois. I also worked at a doughnut shop in Columbia, Missouri. I can put the two together.

Interviewer: We all relate to the things we know about, the things that correspond to us. In that sense, we are all ordinary people.

Alan Gross: The two major things in life to write about are work and family. Freud discusses work and family. He says that is what makes the integrated man. If you can write about work and family, you will write a good piece. We will be interested in reading that. Arthur Miller probably wrote the great American play, *Death of a Salesman.* It's about work and family. The great American novel, to me, is *The Grapes of Wrath* (by John Steinbeck.) It's about work and family. If you can integrate work and family, you've got a leg up. But if you can do just work or just family, you will be fine.

Interviewer: You spend time away from your desk then—researching.

Alan Gross: You should do research. You can get out there and get the feeling. I am not just sitting down at a word processor. As far as I am concerned, you should write with a quill pen. I am interested in the words and the metaphors. I write in longhand, scratch it out, and then I cut and paste it.

I know that William Styron went back to Brooklyn and looked at the house (for *Sophie's Choice*) and thought about it and wrote about it. There are life spaces that he talks about. He talks about the girl who dies in his town when he wrote *Lie Down in Darkness.* He talks about being in the war when he did *The Long March.* He talks about inheriting the land in the South when he did *Nat Turner.* He talks about all the other life spaces that make up all the other books in his life. To read that book (*Sophie's Choice*) and think about Stingo the writer and the life spaces . . . Styron has not kept an exceptional life, but in 56 years he has been in six places where he can build. Writing is active, it isn't passive.[3]

1. Pinpoint elements of Alan Gross's prewriting approaches.

2. Explain his emphasis on work and the family as writing topics.

3. What does he imply about his revision process?

[3]Jill Lewis, "An Interview with Alan Gross," *Writing!* (September 1983), 11–13.

Name _____

Date _____

An Interview with _____

Directions: Using the interviews in **Handout 59** as models, participate in your own interviews about your experiences as a writer. Add to the list of questions provided and write down your interviewee's responses.

Interviewer: _____   **Interviewee:** _____

Interviewer: By now you've had experience with autobiography, third person narration, exposition, description, persuasion, and argumentation. Which modes do you prefer? Why?

Interviewer: How do you get your ideas? What prewriting strategies have you found most enjoyable and helpful?

Interviewer: When and where do you usually do your most successful drafting? Do you use a pen, a pencil, or a word processor?

Interviewer: How do you know when you are ready for conferencing? Who are your best sources for conferencing?

Interviewer: When you revise, what specific concerns do you usually focus on?

Interviewer: What kinds of mistakes do you ordinarily catch and correct in your final draft?

Interviewer: How important to you is the publication of your writing?

Interviewer: Based on your experience, what advice would you give to other young writers?

Lesson 40
The Self-Directed Writer

Objective
- To design and carry out original writing projects

Notes to the Teacher
This lesson encourages students to select their own preferred writing modes, subjects, and audiences. The students devise their own writing projects and implement the six activities that comprise the writing process.

The directions for the projects allow for broad latitude in students' choices. If more specific limits (e.g., number of pages or words) are needed, establish them before students actually begin to work. Make sure that students have a copy of **Handout 62** before they start. The evaluation can be used as an assessment of students' ability to design and carry out original writing projects.

Procedure
1. Use the interviews in Lesson 39 as examples to show that writers select their own approaches. Maya Angelou chooses autobiography over fiction. Charles Leroux opts for the essay instead of the narrative. Alan Gross decides to write a variety of forms rather than just one.

2. Ask students to pause for a moment to consider themselves as writers. Do they prefer to write stories? essays? arguments? Who is their preferred audience? children? peers? adults? What subjects do they really know?

3. Have students read **Handout 61**. Use the Teacher Resource Page as a transparency to share a sample project with the class.

4. Establish a reasonable deadline for students to complete their projects. Direct them to submit their rough draft(s) and completed **Handout 61** along with the final papers. **Handout 62,** an evaluation rubric, can be used to guide and assess the final drafts.

A Sample Project Plan

Step 1. Prewriting
      a. Select your writing mode.
      to convince people

      b. Select your audience.
      general audience of citizens in our town

      c. Select your topic.
      smoking in public places

      d. Devise some strategies that will add to your knowledge or intensify your awareness of the subject.
      observe interactions of smokers and nonsmokers in restaurants and at mall; interview several nonsmokers; research ideas of audience about danger to nonsmokers

Step 2. Drafting
Focus on your subject, your purpose, and your audience.
      a. Where will you write?
      my bedroom

      b. When will you write?
      Tuesday evening from 8 to 9:30

Step 3. Conferencing
Do not skip this step! Helpful feedback is an invaluable tool for discovering the strengths and weaknesses of your work. Self-conferencing can both precede and succeed conferencing with others.
      a. Who will read and react to my work?
      myself, my sister, my uncle

Step 4. Revising
Remember that you do not have to implement all suggestions. You may find it helpful to complete a series of conferencing-revision-conferencing-revision experiences.
      a. What should I focus on during my revision?
      develop analogy for illustration; concrete word choices; overall organization

Step 5. Editing
Watch especially for those errors that tend to slip repeatedly into your writing.
      a. What errors have I found?
      "there" instead of "their"; noun-pronoun inconsistency

Step 6. Publishing
Your mode of publication depends largely on your topic and audience. Your key question is "How can I get this composition to my target audience?"
      a. What is my publication approach?
      youth page of community newspaper

An Original Writing Project

Step 1.   Prewriting
      a. Select your writing mode.

      b. Select your audience.

      c. Select your topic.

      d. Devise some strategies that will add to your knowledge or intensify your awareness of the subject.

Step 2.   Drafting
Focus on your subject, your purpose, and your audience.
      a. Where will you write?

      b. When will you write?

Step 3.   Conferencing
Don't skip this step! Helpful feedback is an invaluable tool for discovering the strengths and weaknesses of your work. Self-conferencing can both precede and succeed conferencing with others.
      a. Who will read and react to my work?

Step 4.   Revising
Remember that you do not have to implement all suggestions. You may find it helpful to complete a series of conferencing-revision-conferencing-revision experiences.
      a. What should I focus on during my revision?

Step 5.   Editing
Watch especially for those errors that tend to slip repeatedly into your writing.
      a. What errors have I found?

Step 6.   Publishing
Your mode of publication depends largely on your topic and audience. Your key question is "How can I get this composition to my target audience?"
      a. What is my publication approach?

Name _____

Date _____

Self-Directed Essay Evaluation

Directions: Each of the following criteria will be given a score. Use this rubric as a guide while completing your assignment.

Criteria		Points	
1.	The style and content suited to the target audience.	_____	/8
2.	The essay expresses and fulfills a purpose.	_____	/8
3.	The writer demonstrates independence and initiative in selecting writing activities.	_____	/8
4.	The writer works within the framework of the selected mode.	_____	/8
5.	The writer expresses and supports a main idea.	_____	/8
6.	The writer demonstrates knowledge of the subject.	_____	/8
7.	Each paragraph has a main idea.	_____	/8
8.	All paragraphs are relevant.	_____	/8
9.	All paragraphs are well-organized.	_____	/8
10.	Transitions are smooth.	_____	/8
11.	The conclusion is clearly stated.	_____	/8
12.	There is evidence of implementation of some conference suggestions.	_____	/8
13.	The mechanics are correct.	_____	/4
14.	There is sentence variety.	_____	/4
15.	Action verbs are used.	_____	/4
16.	Colorful, detailed language is used.	_____	/4
17.	Word economy is used.	_____	/4
	Total points	_____	/116

Comments:

Acknowledgments

For permission to reprint all works in this volume, grateful acknowledgment is made to the following holders of copyright, publishers, or representatives.

Lesson 12, Teacher Resource Page

For use of 5 July 1987 "Peanuts" cartoon. PEANUTS reprinted by permission of United Feature Syndicate, Inc.

Lesson 12, Handout 16

For use of "Alice in Washington" from *I Am Not a Crook* by Art Buchwald, © 1974. Reprinted with the permission of the Roslyn Targ Literary Agency, Inc.

Lesson 12, Handout 17

For use of "The Ghosts of Congresses Past" by Mike Kilian in *The Chicago Tribune* © 1987. Used by permission of The Chicago Tribune.

Lesson 12, Handout 18

For use of "Advice for the Typically Absent-Minded" by Jack R. Robinson from *The Plain Dealer* 29 May 1987. Reprinted by permission of The Plain Dealer and the author.

Lesson 22, Handout 33

For use of excerpt from "Portrait: Old South" in *The Collected Essays and Occasional Writings of Katherine Anne Porter* © 1970. Reprinted by permission of The Permissions Company for the Estate of Katherine Anne Porter.

For use of excerpt from "A Worn Path" in *A Curtain of Green and Other Stories*, copyright 1941 and renewed 1969 by Eudora Welty, reprinted by permission of Harcourt, Inc.

Lesson 24, Handout 35

For use of text from a Subaru of America advertisement for four-wheel drive vehicles. Reprinted with permission from Subaru of America, Inc.

Lesson 24, Handout 36

For use of the text from a Phillips Petroleum advertisement. Reprinted with permission.

For use of the text from a Kellogg's advertisement. *Kellogg's* and *Two Scoops* are trademarks of Kellogg Co. Used with permission.

For use of text from a Northwest Airlines advertisement. Reprinted with permission of Saatchi & Saatchi DFS Compton, New York, New York.

Lesson 31, Procedure 1

For use of the poem "There is no Frigate like a Book" by Emily Dickinson. Reprinted by permission of the publishers and the Trustees of Amherst College from *The Collected Poems of Emily Dickinson*, Ralph W. Franklin, ed., Cambridge, Mass.: The Belknap Press of Harvard University Press, Copyright © 1998 by the President and Fellows of Harvard College. Copyright © 1951, 1955, 1979 by the President and Fellows of Harvard College.

Lesson 31, Handout 48

For use of the poem "Grape Sherbet" by Rita Dove in *Selected Poems*, Random House, 1993. © 1983 by Rita Dove. Reprinted by permission of the author.

For use of the poem "Heart, have no pity on this house of bone" by Edna St. Vincent Millay. From *Collected Poems*, HarperCollins. Copyright © 1931, 1958 by Edna St. Vincent Millay and Norma Millay Ellis. All rights reserved. Reprinted by permission of Elizabeth Barnett, literary executor.

For use of the poems "A Passing Glimpse" and "Nothing Gold Can Stay" from *The Poetry of Robert Frost* edited by Edward Connery Lathem. Copyright 1942, 1951, © 1956 by Robert Frost, © 1970 by Lesley Frost Ballantine, copyright 1923, 1928, 1969 by Henry Holt and Co. Reprinted by permission of Henry Holt and Company, LLC.

Lesson 32, Handout 49

For use of the poem "The Silken Tent" from *The Poetry of Robert Frost* edited by Edward Connery Lathem. Copyright 1942, 1951, © 1956 by Robert Frost, © 1970 by Lesley Frost Ballantine, copyright 1923, 1928, 1969 by Henry Holt and Co. Reprinted by permission of Henry Holt and Company, LLC.

For use of the poem "Love is not all: it is not meat nor drink" by Edna St. Vincent Millay. From *Collected Poems*, HarperCollins. Copyright © 1931, 1958 by Edna St. Vincent Millay and Norma Millay Ellis. All rights reserved. Reprinted by permission of Elizabeth Barnett, literary executor.

Language Arts Series

Advanced Placement

Advanced Placement English 1:
 Practical Approaches to Literary Analysis

Advanced Placement English 2:
 In-depth Analysis of Literary Forms

Advanced Placement Poetry

Advanced Placement Short Story

Advanced Placement Writing 1

Advanced Placement Writing 2

Composition

Advanced Composition
 (Teacher Manual and Student Workbook)

Basic Composition
 (Teacher Manual and Student Workbook)

Creative Writing

Daily Writing Topics

Grammar Mastery—For Better Writing
 (Teacher Guide and Student Workbooks)

Grammar Power—the Essential Elements
 (Teacher Guide and Student Workbook)

Journalism: Writing for Publication

Research 1: Information Literacy

Research 2: The Research Paper

Writing 1: Learning the Process

Writing 2: Becoming a Writer

Writing Short Stories

Writing Skills and the Job Search

Cross-Curriculum

Doing My Part: Reflections on Community
 Service for High School Students (Teacher
 Manual and Student Reflection Handbook)

Peer Mediation:
 Training Students in Conflict Resolution

The Positive Teacher: Daily Reflections

Searching for Yourself

Supervisor/Student Teacher Manual

Valuing Others

Literary Forms

Mythology

Nonfiction: A Critical Approach

Participating in the Poem

Science Fiction—19th Century

Short Poems: Their Vitality and Versatility

The Short Story

Thematic Approaches to British Poetry

Literary Traditions

American Literature 1:
 Beginnings through Civil War

American Literature 2: Civil War to Present

Archetypes in Life, Literature, and Myth

British Literature 1:
 Beginnings to Age of Reason

British Literature 2: Romantics to the Present

Honors American Literature 1:
 Beginnings through Nineteenth Century

Honors American Literature 2:
 World War I to the Present

Multicultural Literature:
 Essays, Fiction, and Poetry

World Literature 1: A Thematic Approach

World Literature 2: A Thematic Approach

Special Topics

Creative Dramatics in the Classroom

Junior High Language Arts

Let's Read! Young Adult Fiction:
 Tools for Individualized Reading Programs,
 Volumes 1 and 2

Let's Read! Classics and Literary Novels:
 Tools for Individualized Reading Programs,
 Volumes 3 and 4

Reading Strategies

Reading Thematically: History Stories

Speech

Thinking, Reading, Writing, Speaking

The Center for Learning

The Publisher

All instructional materials identified by the TAP® (Teachers/Authors/Publishers) trademark are developed by a national network of 460 teacher-authors, whose collective educational experience distinguishes the publishing objective of The Center for Learning, a nonprofit educational corporation founded in 1970.

Concentrating on values-related disciplines, the Center publishes humanities and religion curriculum units for use in public and private schools and other educational settings. Approximately 600 language arts, social studies, novel/drama, life issues, and faith publications are available.

Publications are regularly evaluated and updated to meet the changing and diverse needs of teachers and students. Teachers may offer suggestions for development of new publications or revisions of existing titles by contacting

The Center for Learning
Administration/Creative Development
P.O. Box 417, Evergreen Road
Villa Maria, PA 16155
(800) 767-9090 • FAX (724) 964-1802

The Center for Learning
Editorial/Prepress
24600 Detroit Road, Suite 201
Westlake, OH 44145
(440) 250-9341 • FAX (440) 250-9715

For a free catalog containing order and price information and a descriptive listing of titles, contact

The Center for Learning
Customer Service
P.O. Box 910, Evergreen Road
Villa Maria, PA 16155
(724) 964-8083 • (800) 767-9090
FAX (888) 767-8080
http://www.centerforlearning.org